T3-BPW-452

TELECOMMUNICATIONS
for Local Government

Telecommunications for
Local Government

The International City Management Association is the professional and educational organization for chief appointed management executives in local government. The purposes of
ICMA are to strengthen the quality of urban government
through professional management and to develop and disseminate new approaches to management through training programs, information services, and publications.

Managers, carrying a wide range of titles, serve cities, towns,
counties, and councils of governments in all parts of the
United States and Canada. These managers serve at the direction of elected councils and governing boards. ICMA serves
these managers and local governments through many programs that aim at improving the manager's professional com-
petence and strengthening the quality of all local governments.

The International City Management Association was founded
in 1914; adopted its City Management Code of Ethics in 1924;
and established its Institute for Training in Municipal Administration in 1934. The Institute, in turn, provided the basis for
the Municipal Management Series, generally termed the
"ICMA Green Books."

ICMA's interests and activities include public management
education; standards of ethics for members; the *Municipal
Year Book* and other data services; urban research; and newsletters, a monthly magazine, *Public Management,* and other
publications. ICMA's efforts for the improvement of local government management—as represented by this book—are offered for all local governments and educational institutions.

TELECOMMUNICATIONS
for Local Government

Edited by

Fred S. Knight
International City
Management Association

Harold E. Horn
Cable Television
Information Center

Nancy J. Jesuale
Cable Television
Information Center

International
City
Management
Association

PRACTICAL MANAGEMENT SERIES
Barbara H. Moore, Editor

Library of Congress Cataloging in Publication Data

Main entry under title:
Telecommunications for local government.
    (Practical management series)
    1. Local government—United States
—Communication systems. 2. Govern-
ment communication systems—United
States. I. Knight, Fred S., 1948-   . II.
Horn, Harold E. III. Jesuale, Nancy J. IV.
Series.
JS344.T45T44 1982   352′.000472′0973
82-15617   ISBN 0-87326-036-8

Copyright © 1982 by the International City Management
Association, 1120 G Street, N.W., Washington, D.C.
20005. All rights reserved, including rights of
reproduction and use in any form or by any means,
including the making of copies by any photographic
process, or by any electronic or mechanical device,
printed or written or oral, or recording for sound or visual
reproduction, or for use in any knowledge or retrieval
system or device, unless permission in writing is obtained
from the copyright proprietor.

Printed in the United States of America.
12345 • 8988878685848382

Foreword

The telecommunications technology of the "Information Age" is rapidly overtaking local government. Cable communications, enhanced and interactive services, new telephone systems—all pose questions that demand knowledge and action on the parts of local decision makers and citizens.

Telecommunications for Local Government presents readings that describe these and other technologies, that explain how local governments are using them, and that offer guidelines for telecommunications planning. The book also examines the issues, such as privacy and antitrust, that must be considered simultaneously with decisions about implementing these new services.

This is the first book in ICMA's Practical Management Series, devoted to serving local officials' needs for timely information on current issues and problems. The editors have drawn on ICMA publications, professional journals, industry literature, consultants, and other sources to bring a wealth of material to the reader's hands.

We are grateful to Harold Horn and Nancy Jesuale of the Cable Television Information Center for their participation in this project; to Bill Henderson and Randy Young of Henderson, Young & Company and F. L. Smith, Jr., of AT&T, who wrote articles for the book; and to the organizations that granted ICMA permission to reprint their material. David S. Arnold, Editor, Municipal Management Series, was of great help in planning for this book and the entire Practical Management Series.

Mark E. Keane
Executive Director
International City
    Management Association

Preface

Everyone seems to be talking about telecommunications these days. Whether it's a neighbor-to-neighbor discussion on the pros and cons of subscribing to cable, teen-agers (and more than a few adults) spending their spare quarters in the local video arcade, employee conversation around the office water cooler about pending changes in the organization's phone system, or friendly giants such as IBM, Xerox, and Wang promoting hardware configurations that portend the restructuring of business and office practices—it is virtually impossible for today's local government managers and the citizens they serve to ignore the early manifestations of the telecommunications revolution. The "Information Age" so long predicted by futurists, scholars, and the information industry itself appears finally to have arrived.

But if a new day has indeed dawned, what does it mean to the millions of men and women who work with and for local governments? It is ICMA's hope that this book of readings will help local government officials and employees seize the initiative and begin to consider their organization from a new perspective—in terms of telecommunications.

Telecommunications, in the context of local government, typically includes telephone systems, cable systems, automated office equipment, and—central to those three technologies—the computer. When viewed individually, each technology has the potential for altering the process by which local governments receive, transmit, or store information. When viewed collectively, these technologies have the potential for altering work patterns and habits, breaking down traditional office hierarchies, and changing the manner in which local officials communicate with the citizenry they serve.

It is unlikely, however, that sweeping changes will overtake local government officials overnight. The technology may be changing rapidly, but the intelligent integration of new hardware systems and management structures into municipal organizations will require time, careful planning, and testing. Moreover, the rapid changes within the industries themselves—for example, the rapid evolution of the cable industry from a "mom-and-pop" business into one dominated by a few still-developing conglomerates, and the emergence of new competitors to AT&T—make it difficult to know which companies (and therefore which companies' promises) to view with confidence.

Local government officials can gain confidence in applying telecommunications only if they undertake a thorough examination of how their organizations work. They need to identify who communicates with whom, and for what reasons; examine how information is stored and received; and pinpoint the information needs of elected officials, staff, and citizens that go unfulfilled because of outmoded technology. This planning process itself is not new to municipal officials. What is new is its application to telecommunications in a local government setting.

There is no standard, tried-and-tested telecommunications planning methodology for use in local governments today. But this book includes examples of what local governments are doing and provides a basis for adapting the experiences of others based on a community's needs and resources.

This book also contains the perspective of the industries—particularly the cable industry. While "industry gossip" has been edited out as much as possible, the intent is to share with public sector consumers of telecommunications services what the industry is saying to itself relative to the viability of many highly touted nonentertainment services. Other perspectives are presented as well, and it should be pointed out that all opinions are those of the authors of the respective articles and are not necessarily statements of ICMA policy.

The reader will also note that this book is weighted heavily toward cable and general telecommunications planning, with a moderate size section on telephone and much less on satellites and microwave. To examine the entire spectrum of telecommunications technologies and associated issues in detail goes beyond the scope of one book. (Related topics are under consideration for future volumes in this Practical Management Series.) This book represents an attempt to describe nonentertainment services, the issues associated with those services, and some of the potential delivery systems for those services. It is our hope that the reader will forgive these self-imposed constraints and that new knowledge and information will be derived from what is included.

The central fact concerning telecommunications is that it is a harbinger—indeed, a guarantor—of change. Whether the change is for good or ill, what it portends for our nation's cities and counties, and for the citizens who reside therein, is in the hands of local officials and the decisions those officials make today. The more they know about the technologies, and the more thought they give to the implications of using them in their organizations and communities, the more likely it is that the technologies can be harnessed for good. This book is intended to be both informative and thought-provoking. It is our sincere hope that those goals have been achieved.

Fred S. Knight

About the Editors

Fred S. Knight is Senior Staff Associate at the International City Management Association. Since joining ICMA in 1974, he has directed and managed the association's technical assistance and research programs to apply science and technology to local government problems. A former administrative assistant to the city coordinator in Minneapolis, Mr. Knight holds a B.A. degree from the University of Minnesota and an M.P.A. degree from the Maxwell School, Syracuse University.

Harold E. Horn is President, Cable Television Information Center. He also has served as the Center's deputy director and director of field services and was responsible for overseeing the provision of technical assistance to local governments. As president, he manages and directs consulting and research activities and monitors the development of telecommunications issues that affect local governments. Mr. Horn has served as associate director of ICMA and as manager of Lawrence and Concordia, Kansas. He holds an A.B. degree from Baker University and an M.P.A. from the University of Kansas.

Nancy J. Jesuale is Director of Public Information for the Cable Television Information Center, editor of the CTIC *CableReports*, and co-editor of the *CTIC Cablebooks*. She directs the Center's nonprofit services to local officials, including publishing, seminars, and research activities. Since 1976, she has been involved with cable franchising, programming, and production. Ms. Jesuale holds a B.A. degree from Goucher College.

Contents

PART 1
Overview

The Birth of a Wired Nation   3
   Ralph Lee Smith
Overview of Cable TV Services and Technology   13
   Nancy J. Jesuale and Ralph Lee Smith
Telecommunications in the Year 2000   21
   Joseph P. Martino

PART 2
Enhanced Services

Cable Stakes Claim to Unmined Markets   35
   Jeri Baker
Getting Ready for Videotex, Teletext and the
Interactive Worlds Beyond   42
   Gary Arlen
Enhanced and Interactive Services   51
   Janet Quigley
Security and Fire Alarm Services   62
   John Mansell
A New Institution   68
   Victoria Gits
Institutional Networks   75
   Thomas E. Wolfsohn
Planning for the Use of Cable in Municipal
Services   87
   Fred S. Knight

PART 3
Community Programming

A Different Kind of Television   105
   Jim Bell
Improving Local Community Access
Programming   111
   Sue Miller Buske

PART 4
Telephone Systems

System Diagnosis: How to Evaluate Your
Telephone System   119
   Paul Daubitz and Robert Ross

Telecommunications in Your Future: A Manager's
Planning Guide   136
    F. L. Smith, Jr.
Choice or Chance: Managing Procurement for
Telephone Systems   149
    Bill Henderson and Randy Young

PART 5
Satellite and Other
Advanced Technologies

Beware the Killer Birds   165
    Jonathan Miller
The 'Un' Wired Nation? MDS Makes Its Case   169
    Don Franco
Rewiring America   173
    Morris Edwards

PART 6
Emerging Issues: Privacy,
Antitrust, and Interconnection

Privacy and Cable: How Severe the Problem?   181
    Richard M. Neustadt
The Twists in Two-Way Cable   186
    David Burnham
The Boulder Decision   192
    Howard J. Gan
Vital Links: Interconnection of Cable Systems   208
    Linda J. Camp

PART 1

Overview

The Birth of a Wired Nation

Ralph Lee Smith

In May 1970, Ralph Lee Smith's article in The Nation *attracted wide interest for its assertion that the United States would soon be substantially wired from coast to coast for cable television. Entitled* The Wired Nation, *the article not only covered the social potential of the intriguing new medium but also the policy questions it raised. In 1972, an expanded version of the article was published as a book by Harper & Row. However, when cable faltered in its first attempts to penetrate the major cities, its glamor evaporated, and Smith's prediction was dismissed like an erroneous weather forecast.*

Now the picture has changed. Cable has begun to spread rapidly across the country, as was predicted a decade ago. Here, Smith takes a fresh look at cable, assesses its development, and reexamines his earlier conclusions.

The future arrived officially on the 18th of May, 1980, the day the National Cable Television Association convention opened in Dallas. History was not so much made at this event as marked by it. Scores of people not directly involved in the cable industry—financiers, corporation executives, producers, city government officials, and journalists—were drawn to the convention by a powerful sense that something momentous was happening in America. Whether or not they thought about it in these terms, they had made their pilgrimage to Dallas to witness the birth of the New Age of Television.

Reprinted with permission from *Channels of Communications*, April/May 1981. © Media Commentary Council, Inc. This article will appear in a book entitled *The New Television*, to be released in the spring of 1983. Research for this article was funded in part by the Fund for Investigative Journalism.

It was clear that America was on the threshold of becoming a "wired nation," that in the next few years homes and offices all across the country would be equipped for cable television, the rapidly expanding technology that creates dozens of new channels in each community, foreseeably as many as, or more than, fifty.

Old ideas about broadcasting for mass audiences are rendered obsolete by this profusion of television channels. They can potentially break the lock-step of existing commercial television; they can bring a greater variety of informational, educational, and cultural viewing material to the home screen, and can serve the needs of communities, smaller audiences, and special groups. They lend themselves also to new forms of communications services, such as the transmission of textual material, pay television, and home security systems. Cable promises, at once, a television renaissance and tantalizing opportunities for new wealth.

The new networks, pay services, and technical devices introduced at the Dallas convention all reflected the robustness of the industry and signified that cable was now truly, after several tentative starts, on the move across the land. The communications revolution that began incongruously in rural areas and small towns was expanding its programming store as it was beginning to sweep the cities. During the next three or four years virtually every major metropolitan market will be franchised for cable. Well before the end of this decade the United States will be a wired nation. And when this wiring is done, things will never be quite the same again.

It must be said, however, that costs prohibit the country's ever becoming *completely* wired. Large geographical areas—the sparsely settled countryside between urban centers—will probably never have cable because the cost of "laying hard wire" is so great that no company could find it profitable to build systems there. The American Broadcasting Companies Inc. was probably correct when it estimated, in 1975 testimony before a Senate subcommittee, that the cost of wiring half the country would be $10 billion—and the cost for the other half $250 billion.

The portions of the country not covered by cable are likely to be served instead by satellites broadcasting directly to homes, and by the newly authorized low-power television stations. One way or another, these areas will also experience an explosion of channels, and will thus share in the bounty of the wired nation.

Who will control these powerful new communications systems, and how much should government regulate them? Who will have access rights to cable and how should they be used? What material should be allowed into American homes? Is it healthy for the parties who control the program sources to operate the cable systems through which they are delivered?

Should telephone companies be allowed to operate cable systems and thereby deliver both telephone and television over a single wire? If so, should the federal government regulate—or should the municipality? What should the new rules be? Finally, as companies frantically scramble for cable franchises in the large cities, are they promising more than they can possibly deliver? And if they don't deliver, how may city governments and the public legally respond?

History

Cable was a long time coming. Its function in the early fifties was to bring in a clear television picture and a greater selection of over-the-air television channels to areas of poor reception. The excitement over cable came with the discovery that the wire could provide channels in far greater number than the airwaves could, and that these channels might be used for a good deal more than light entertainment. For its social service potential, the new medium caught the fancy of social scientists, urban planners, community organizers, educators, and video enthusiasts. But most of them gave up on it when their ideas did not bear fruit overnight.

In 1975, Home Box Office (HBO), a small pay-television service, made a fateful decision to hitch its future to the RCA Satcom I satellite. Cable's resurgence traces to that single action, for what HBO achieved in transmitting its signal by satellite was an instant national network, one with distribution capabilities resembling those of ABC, CBS, and NBC, but at a fraction of the cost. Other companies quickly followed HBO's lead.[1]

Because it carried HBO (the most popular service), RCA's Satcom I became the main satellite for cable. In short order its twenty channels were claimed, and some have been subleased to programmers at handsome profits. Many prospective users are waiting for space, and others have booked transponders on Western Union's Westar satellite in hopes that cable systems would build a second earth station to take down its signals.

Cable services

In addition to the shower of programming pouring from the satellite, cable has gained from technology such new applications as fire- and burglar-alarm systems; two-way communications capabilities that make shopping, banking, and polling possible by cable; and the use of the home television screen as a display terminal for printed information. Also, some cable systems are building special local networks to facilitate interchanges of visual materials and data between schools, hospitals, libraries, and municipal offices. The cable operator in 1980 therefore has what he lacked in the 1970s—important things to sell in the major cities. And this has incited the wild rush for big city franchises.

The systems that cable companies now propose to build in the large urban markets differ markedly from those constructed in the past. As early as 1963, twelve-channel cable came into regular use in rural areas. It remained standard until the early seventies, when new twenty-channel systems were built.

By the end of 1979, 70 percent of all existing U.S. cable systems still had not changed their 12-channel programming capacity. In new franchise offerings, however, channel capacity has rapidly climbed from forty to fifty-two, and in some cases, to more than one hundred. Virtually all bidders now offer the two-way and pay-per-program capabilities.

Subscribers can now buy new programming in several differently priced tiers of basic service. Typical tiers include combinations of over-the-air signals; satellite-delivered programming; informational, educational, and cultural material, and local-access channels. Cable has moved so far from its position of five years ago that today some companies give away their initial tier of basic service (which used to be cable's economic mainstay). Subscribers to this new-style cable system may pay anywhere from nothing to $50 monthly for the services they select.

Such sophisticated cable systems are terribly expensive to construct. The wiring costs for cities like Cincinnati, St. Paul, and Omaha, with system sizes ranging from 110,000 to 160,000 homes, are expected to run up to $40 million. Dallas, with 400,000 homes, will cost $100 million.

Franchises

Despite such costs, with the vast array of programming and services, few people doubt that high-capacity cable systems can be built and operated profitably in urban centers. But there remains a major question: Has the medium already been crippled by furious franchise competition, in which bids must offer immense cash giveaways and low subscriber fees?

Since early 1979, bids on franchises have gone berserk: eighty or more channels of programming for just $10 a month; immediate prepayment to the municipality of the franchise fee in the amount of millions of dollars; purchasing of bonds issued by financially destitute municipalities; building and equipping of access centers; funding of foundations to support local programming; creation of tape libraries, and granting of substantial equity in the entire venture to people with political influence, to local civic groups, or to a city itself.

Obviously, this is not a game for the faint-hearted or cautious. Cities and cable companies blame each other for the current craziness. Monroe Rifkin, president of American Television and Communications Corporation (ATC), has said that the cable franchising process occurs in an environment "where excesses are encouraged and realism is penalized." David Korte of the Cable Television Information Center, a nonprofit group that advises cities, put the shoe on the other foot. "The applicants are promising not only more than the city wants, but more than they are capable of delivering." It is not evident that cities are unhappy with the giveaway offers made by franchisees. But many do believe unrealistic promises are being made. If the promises cannot be kept, everyone stands to be harmed. As the highly respected journal, *Cable TV Regulation Newsletter,* said in August 1980, "Just when you think franchising competition has peaked and there is nothing left to offer, another summit is sighted and a new crest must be scaled. The future breathing space for a reasonable rate of return seems to be thinning."

Economics

Reviewing the six applications submitted for the Dallas franchise, the Cable Television Information Center criticized them all for not showing an adequate rate of return, which is most simply defined as the money a corporation has made on its capital investment after expenses and taxes have been paid. The financial consulting firm of Gary A. Dent Associates, analyzing the same Dallas bids and taking the bidders' own figures at face value, reported that, after twelve years of operations, rates of return on the projected investments for the entire period ran from 4.74 percent down to minus 5.32 percent, with three of the six bids showing rates of return of less than zero. Even if the system were sold after twelve years of operations, Dent figures indicated that the rate of return for all the bidders would be significantly less than the current cost of borrowing money. This approach is risky for any venture. But what makes the high-cost cable situation particularly alarming is the fact that the service is being so blithely merchandised, and its anticipated revenues so cheerfully totted up even before results are in. No cable system comparable to the type now being franchised has been built anywhere before. Both its costs and its potential dwarf those of existing systems. In addition, the demographics of the urban centers receiving the new cable are, generally, very different from the demographics of the medium-sized and small towns that until recently have been cable's principal market.

The limited amount of market experience gained in these smaller systems is not a reliable guide to the economics of big-city "supercable." No one really knows what services and offerings the subscriber to the new urban cable system will actually pay for.

Competition

Another complicating factor is that cable's rank among the electronic technologies to be unleashed on the American consumer in the eighties has not been fully established. Technologies that may compete for at least part of the cable subscriber's time and dollar include video tape and video disk, direct broadcasting from satellite to home (DBS), and multipoint distribution service (MDS).

The last may be a real sleeper. MDS is a microwave common-carrier broadcasting technology that can disseminate television signals within a twenty-mile radius. Current FCC rules permit MDS stations to transmit two television channels in urban centers. MDS signals are principally beamed to hotels, motels, and business establishments, although operators have begun to solicit home hook-ups for the delivery of pay television. To receive MDS one must install a small microwave receiving dish and down-converter that cost around $250.

It takes $30 million to $100 million to bring cable to urban centers; MDS stations can be built and put on the air in the same areas for about $100,000. Moreover, there is no serious technical reason why the MDS transmission band could not be expanded for twenty or thirty television signals. Because it is a broadcasting technology MDS is regulated entirely at the federal level, so the local franchising situation has no effect on its installation. MDS operations can be established in any city, whether or not a cable system exists there.

Another competitor for some viewers is low-powered television broadcasting. This service, for which the FCC is now processing applications, will involve the licensing of hundreds of highly localized television stations throughout the country, each transmitting over relatively short distances. A 1978 FCC Task Force estimated that the cost of creating such a station, complete with minimal program origination facilities, would be $55,000. Low-powered stations are capable of providing many kinds of television service, including pay television.

Reforming the process

To introduce high-cost cable into this volatile scene—especially with commitments that push projected rates of return to the vanishing point—is risky, to say the least. The cable franchising process needs to be greatly reformed, so that the public and private risks can be substantially reduced. It would be wise to curb the lavish giveaway promises made against unknown returns and to delay the introduction of new technology until it has undergone extensive market experimentation. Overall, there is a need for intelligent planning.

Unfortunately, each of those who could lead reform—city governments, access groups, and consumer advocates—stands to lose some of the cable operator's largesse if the system were to be improved. Most prefer the giveaways being offered to a more orderly and reasonable franchising procedure.

A front-page article in the March 10, 1980, issue of *access*, the publication of Ralph Nader's National Citizens Committee for Broadcasting, summarized the current mood in making these recommendations for local action:

1. "Ask for twice as many local channels as the cable company offers;
2. "exact a high franchise fee;
3. "find out what is available in the finest cable systems today, and then ask for more."

Now that cable companies are realizing that local access groups will be making substantial demands, those companies are incorporating high-cost access projects, with large staffs, into their proposals.

By joining—and, in fact, leading—the every-man-for-himself melee that now passes for national policy on cable, groups wearing the mantle of the public interest look more like part of the difficulty than part of the solution. The essential problem is the absence of any national policy on cable.

There are two well-established objectives of the United States communications policy. The first is *establishment of a strong national pattern of communications.* The Communications Act of 1934, which created the FCC, states that the Commission was formed:

for the purpose of regulating interstate and foreign commerce and communication by wire and radio so as to make available, so far as possible, to all people of the United States, a rapid, efficient, nationwide, and worldwide wire and radio communications service with adequate facilities at reasonable charges.

The second goal of communications policy, reflected in many of the FCC proceedings, is *the promotion of communications capabilities at the local level.* This objective was well stated by the President's 1968 Task Force on Communications Policy:

No aspect of communications policy is more important than measures or arrangements which would permit or encourage the growth of communications of all kinds within localities: the discussion of local issues; contact with local or regional political leaders; tapping local talent; the use of local resources in education, technology, sports, and the expression of all kinds of local interests.

Cable is capable of contributing much toward the realization of both these objectives, but the size and value of its contribution depends on how some urgent questions will be dealt with. Who will run these powerful communications systems, who will supervise, and for whose benefit? Who will have access rights to cable, for what purposes and for the transmission of what kinds of material? Who will be turned away?

When I wrote *The Wired Nation* in 1970, I urged Congress to designate cable a common carrier, like the telephone system, satellite systems, and multipoint distribution service. Under this kind of regulation, owners of cable systems would forgo all right to program them. Instead, they would lease channel time to all those who want to present programs, and the leasing would be done on a non-discriminatory basis at standard posted rates. Cable would be available on the same first-come, first-served basis as the telephone. The cable system's owner would have no right to refuse any law-abiding customer. Everyone would have the right to be a cable broadcaster.

My proposal aroused a great deal of interest but produced no action. Now it may be too late to institute such a policy. In many large cities, cable franchises have already been granted with the understanding that the operator will choose the program networks and pay-television services the system will provide and that the operator will share in the proceeds from these services. Since the economic plan of these systems has been worked out on that basis, to drastically change the rules now would create chaos. Yet it is alarming that after all these years there still exists no mandate or structure to help determine a standard for access rights to cable.

All that had served as a structure were rules adopted by the FCC in 1972 requiring all new cable systems in urban centers to set aside one channel each for educational, governmental, and public use at no charge. Also required was a "leased access" channel on which the operator could sell time segments. But these rules were overturned by the federal courts in 1978 on the ground that no adequate basis for them existed in the Communications Act of 1934. The decision abrogated the federal government's right to require either commercial or noncommercial access to cable under existing law.

This leaves the matter up to Congress, but tides running in the national legislature appear to favor less, rather than more, government power to mandate access.

Ownership

Ownership patterns pose another crucial set of questions. For example, the three major pay-television suppliers—Home Box Office, Showtime, and The Movie Channel—have ownership ties with large MSOs, the multiple-system operators of cable. All three are also affiliated with program production companies—The Movie Channel with Warner Bros. TV, Showtime with Viacom Enterprises, and HBO with Time-Life Films. A fourth pay network, Rainbow, was recently established by another group of MSOs. So each of these four enterprises consists of a national supplier of pay programming and a large group of captive cable systems to which the programming can be distributed. Four of the top five—six of the top ten—big cable companies in the United States are involved in these combines.

As cable comes to the cities, power is being consolidated by companies that are already large and already heavily involved in ownership and programming. Since the courts have ruled that the FCC has no power to require access to cable, these companies are free to do as they wish about granting access on their cable systems to new competitors in the programming field. Even where access is granted, the combine controls the marketing of all programming and services. It would not likely promote the programming of a strong competitor if that meant helping the rival make a dent in the national marketplace.

Interestingly, the arrangements now being left to take root in the cable industry bear strong resemblance to the arrangement the government outlawed for movie companies. In the film industry's earlier days, several of the major film studios also owned large theater chains. They used this marriage of exhibition and distribution to control ticket prices and so exclude competing films from their theaters. In 1948 a Justice Department consent decree put an end to such ownership arrangements, forcing the movie studios to divest themselves of theater chains. Now, through the new electronic media, the centralized control of programming, distribution, and exhibition is sneaking back into the marketplace.

Cable and telephone

Yet another issue in the coming of the wired nation, and perhaps the most enigmatic of all, is the role to be played by the telephone company. Ma Bell, the world's largest corporation—and, as a matter of interest, the world's largest common carrier—is at present not involved in cable. The FCC ruled in 1970 that telephone companies cannot build and operate cable systems in areas they provide with telephone service, except in rural situations where telephone company construction is the only feasible alternative.

However, with their tremendous switching capability (which can be applied to two-way cable communications), and with their increasing experience in laying and operating fiber-optic cable, telephone companies are obviously capable of building high capacity cable systems anywhere. Indeed, some people may consider it desirable to have one wire coming into the home—carrying both telephone and cable—rather than two.

The real question is not technological but philosophical. Should Ma Bell be allowed to bring its massive economic power and leverage into this field? If so, under what kind of regulation and with what restrictions?

These questions are not likely to be raised by the American Telephone & Telegraph Company, which has repeatedly said it has no interest in entering the field of cable television. The parties most likely to pose them are the elected officials of some large city at some not-too-distant moment. Weary of franchising battles and giveaways, uncertain whether the offers they receive now will prove financially unrealistic later—or disillusioned to find, after granting a franchise, that the company can't or won't deliver what it promised—the officials in such a city may petition the FCC for something new: that AT&T be licensed to build and operate a common-carrier cable system in their city, something it could accomplish quickly. If and when that happens, how should the government respond?

Regulation

Just when such issues are being pushed more urgently to the forefront of the public agenda by cable's growth, Washington is caught up in the new doctrine of deregulation. The prevailing idea in the capital today is that commerce is better regulated by the marketplace than by government bureaucrats. This has prompted the FCC to disband its Cable Television Bureau and abandon most of its regulatory structure for cable.

As with all philosophies of public policy, deregulation has merit and important uses but tends to be overapplied. It is too easily used in place of thought and planning. And it is notably inapplicable to cable because, as a practical matter, deregulation cannot be achieved by removing only the federal presence. This is because two additional levels of regulation—state and local—lie between cable television and the marketplace. Cancellation of the federal role merely shifts responsibility to the states and municipalities, where there is neither the mandate nor the equipment to formulate rules with a view to the national interest.

If cable is to grow sensibly and in ways that contribute to national communications goals, the responsibility falls to the Congress and the President of the United States.

1. HBO's historical role in cable's resurgence is detailed in [the April/May 1981 issue of *Chan-* *nels*] in Martin Koughan's article, "Playing 'The New Television' at Table Stakes."

Overview of Cable TV Services and Technology

Nancy J. Jesuale and Ralph Lee Smith

Cable television has become an object of fascination to millions of Americans. But to local government decisionmakers, cable television franchising and regulation have become major policy issues. Local governments and private citizens are beginning to realize that cable television means far more to a community than hundreds of entertainment channels. Cable is one part of a growing number of technologies that will make the "information age" a reality. As travel becomes more expensive, as consumers become more educated about computer and satellite technology, and as energy costs and efficiency become standards by which we measure out time and activities, all of us must come to grips with the potential effects of the increasingly "wired nation."

Cable television is a regulated industry. The frantic pace at which cable has been growing has caused Federal and local decisionmakers to seriously consider the public policy issues associated with its implementation: Is cable a monopoly? Should it be used to provide social services? How should it be regulated? Can it compete with other communications technologies? The answers to these questions are not easy to find. On both the Federal and local levels, our Nation's communications policy is in a state of flux. Policymakers are trying both to direct technology and to keep up with it.

In a way, the technological explosion of which cable television is only a part can be likened to the advent of the printing press. For the first time, Gutenberg made it possible for all

Reprinted with permission from *The Community Medium*, volume 1 of *CTIC Cablebooks*, edited by Nancy Jesuale with Ralph Lee Smith (Arlington, Va.: Cable Television Information Center, 1982).

people to learn to read, write, and share information. The information age, in which cable connects to computers, satellites, databases, and telephones, may allow us all to make a quantum leap in the amount of information we can access and the knowledge we can gain.

Right now so little information is available about cable that it tends to be viewed as a novelty, a toy, or merely as a source of entertainment. Many decisionmakers, entrepreneurs, and technologists, however, believe that cable is no more a toy than the first rocket. It is instead, a profound new electronic highway that sends and delivers a diverse and expanded universe of information and images.

Cable television services

Cable television began as a retransmission service; that is, it brought better reception of over-the-air broadcast television signals to communities that did not experience clear reception. When the Federal Communications Commission (FCC) began to regulate cable television, cable was an "ancillary service to broadcasting." Thus, the FCC requires cable operators to transmit all local broadcasting stations and any "significantly viewed stations," including network affiliates, independent stations, and educational stations located within a certain radius of a community. Usually, in 12-channel cable systems, these "must-carry" rules require operators to fill most of their usable channels with local signals. A few channels are usually left over, however, and can be used for other types of services. In systems with 20, 35, 54, or 100 or more channels, the services beyond retransmission of broadcast signals are the economic backbone of cable service.

Basic service   Basic service generally refers to cable services available to the subscriber for one monthly fee. Basic service packages can differ for each cable system. In systems with a large channel capacity (35 channels or more), several "tiers" of basic service are often available, each offering more services for slightly higher monthly fees. Basic service always includes the must-carry signals and often also includes community programming channels and some satellite-delivered programming.

Community programming generally refers to two broad types of programming: access and local origination. Access programming is produced and controlled by some community entity besides the cable operator, who simply makes facilities and channel space available for its transmission. Local origination, on the other hand, is operator-sponsored community programming and is usually more commercial than access programming.

Both types of community programming, however, are uniquely local, and for the most part are carried only on the local cable system. This type of programming is distinct from broadcasting in that no one but cable subscribers can receive it and it is designed to be of special interest to the community.

Satellite-delivered basic services differ from pay TV in that the subscriber does not pay extra to receive them. Many types of satellite services are available to cable operators, and analysts expect even more to appear in the next few years. Satellite program services will face tremendous competition for space even on systems with more than 100 channels.

Satellite-delivered basic services include cable news networks, arts and cultural services, religious programming, children's channels, sports channels, newswire services, public service networks, congressional coverage, weather, and "superstations." Superstations are conventional broadcast stations that use satellites to disseminate their signals far beyond their local coverage area. Superstations are available to local cable systems from Atlanta, New York, and Chicago.

Pay programming Pay programming describes services available to the subscriber for an additional fee over the basic rate. Currently, there are two categories of pay TV: channels available for an additional fee, and "pay-per-view" programs, in which the operator charges the subscriber per program rather than per channel. Perhaps the best-known pay services are the movie channels, which usually offer uncut first-run movies 24 hours a day. The subscriber pays anywhere from $6.50 to $10 per channel for each pay TV service. Pay channels have also been formed to deliver Broadway musicals and other cultural programs, sports, foreign language channels, family entertainment, and adult movies. Some pay channels are considered "maxipays" in that they offer more hours of programming for a higher fee, and some are called "mini-pays," which usually offer fewer hours of family-oriented entertainment for a lower rate. Most pay programming is delivered to the cable system by satellite.

Pay-per-view services are relatively new. The operator usually advertises the program, such as a championship fight or a rock concert, to subscribers. To view the program, the subscriber places an order with the operator on a program-by-program basis. Only households that have requested the program will be able to see it; the signal is "scrambled" or "trapped" to all other homes.

Enhanced and interactive services Some new cable television services use the inherent capacity of coaxial wire to deliver "nonentertainment" services to subscribers. Shop at home, bank at home, home security, videotex, teletext, and subscriber polling services are a few examples of the new enhanced services currently under development in the cable industry. Videotex and teletext services allow the subscriber to access databases that contain information on a variety of subjects, from stock market prices to library catalogs. Teletext is a one-way service, which allows subscribers to "grab" information off a carousel of text pages transmitted through the system. Videotex is a two-way system in which the subscriber keys in a specific request for information that the computer then transmits individually. Other articles describe these and other cable television services and technology in detail.

A cable technology primer

At the heart of cable technology is the cable itself. Coaxial cable looks, in cross-section, like a pencil. In the center is a copper or copper-clad wire. This wire is surrounded by an insulating layer of polyethylene foam, analogous to the wooden cylinder of the pencil. This layer of insulation is surrounded by an aluminum tubular shielding. The entire cable is sheathed in a rubberized outer casing.

When an electronic current is introduced into the cable, the copper wire in the center and the outside shielding react electronically with each other, setting up a magnetic field between them. This field inhibits frequency loss and is the key to cable's immense carrying capacity.

Telephone lines also carry electronic information into the home. However, the pair of wires that deliver telephone service do not create between them a magnetic field of the type generated in a coaxial cable, and their carrying capacity is therefore a tiny fraction of that of coaxial cable.

Bandwidth channel capacity   Carrying capacity is expressed in bandwidth, which means the amount of frequency spectrum that the system can accommodate to transmit signals. Bandwidth, in turn, is expressed in cycles per second, called hertz.

The amount of bandwidth required to transmit television pictures is much greater than the amount required to carry either voice or data. The ordinary home telephone provides clearly intelligible voice transmission with a bandwidth of about three kilohertz.[1] In contrast, a bandwidth of six megahertz is required to transmit a single television picture—2,000 times as much bandwidth as is used to transmit the human voice by telephone.

The term "broadband" is used to describe technologies that can transmit a broad frequency spectrum. As such, they can carry moving television (video) pictures as well as voice and data. Broadband technologies include over-the-air TV broadcasting, cable, satellite, microwave, and fiber optics. "Narrowband" technologies have a more limited frequency range. They can transmit nonvisual material such as voice and data but cannot transmit moving video pictures.

Cable systems being built in major cities and metropolitan areas are often dual-cable facilities; that is, two cables are laid side by side. The carrying capacity of these cables is a function of the associated hardware and various technological considerations. The latest generation of hardware offers some 440 MHz of bandwidth with a practical carrying capacity of 50 to 54 television channels. A dual cable facility would thus provide total capacity of slightly more than 100 television channels. Dedicating even a modest amount of such capacity to data or voice transmission would provide immense capacity for this type of transmission because data and voice use only a fraction of the frequency space that television signals require.

Cable system components   Cable systems have a facility called the *headend* that receives all of the system's programming from various sources, including standard over-the-air TV and radio signals, distant TV and radio signals microwaved to the headend, satellite transmission, videotapes, and material originated in the cable company's local studio. At the headend, signals are amplified and processed, assigned to frequencies on the cable, and transmitted over the cable to the subscribers.

The cable runs through the community on poles or in underground conduit space leased from the telephone or the electric company. The main cable is called the *trunk*. Smaller diameter cable, called *feeder* cable, carries the signals from the trunk into local areas and neighborhoods. *Drop* cables, of yet smaller diameter, run from the feeder cable to individual homes.

From the time that the signals leave the headend, they lose quality and strength as they pass down the cable. *Amplifiers* must be placed at regular intervals along the cable, at spacings of one or two per mile, to bring the signal back up to strength. These amplifiers cannot, however, restore any quality that the signals have lost, and in fact contribute to the degradation of the quality of the signal because passage through any electronic device has a slightly deleterious effect on signal quality. The numerous tapoffs from the feeder cables to subscriber homes also adversely affect the quality of the signals that pass beyond each tapoff to homes farther down the line. These considerations place a maximum limit of about eight to ten miles on the distance that the cable can travel to a subscriber and still transmit pictures of good quality.

Many franchised jurisdictions, of course, have areas that exceed the maximum good signal reach of the cable. This problem is solved by creating a number of hubs, or sub-head-ends, each serving subscribers for a maximum of some eight to ten miles. The hubs are connected to the main headend by a direct cable ("super trunk"), which, because it is not branched or tapped, transmits the signals from the headend to the hub with little loss of quality. In some instances, the hubs are connected to the headend by microwave.

Microwave   Microwave is a special radio frequency set aside by the FCC for closed communications. Often cable operators use microwave rather than trunk cable to traverse long distances. Microwave is often more economical than coaxial cable for extending the coverage area of a system. The cable system signal is beamed via a microwave transmitting antenna to a corresponding microwave receiver and passed along the cable system from the receiving end. Thus, in a hub system, microwave may be used to interconnect the hubs of a system. However, microwave technology is useful only where "line-of-sight" transmitting can be achieved. This is because radio frequency travels in a straight path through the air and is therefore useless where tall buildings, hills, or other obstructions may block the transmission path.

Microwave has also been used to deliver premium or other programming services on a regional basis or in conjunction with satellite technology. The use of microwave to send and receive signals usually depends on the number of channels to be transmitted (microwave has a much more limited channel capacity than does cable), the distance to be traveled, any obstructions, and relative costs. Microwave is more feasible than cable where a long hop is necessary, and line-of-sight transmission can be achieved.

Channel layout for the subscriber network   In a subscriber network cable that can transmit 50 to 55 channels of TV, most of the capacity is usually dedicated to "downstream" transmission from the headend to the subscriber. In modern two-way systems, however, a small portion of the spectrum in the "low-band" range—about 5 to 30 MHz—is usually reserved for "upstream" transmission, from various locales around the community to the headend.

This portion of the spectrum does not provide the highest quality transmission and is subject to interference from citizens' band (CB) and amateur radio signals, which transmit in the same frequency range. Still, several usable video channels, plus a large number of usable voice and data channels, usually can be transmitted on the low-band cable frequencies. The video channels are often used to transmit material from selected fixed sites, such as libraries, community-based access studios, or college and university studios, to the headend for live retransmission downstream on the subscriber network.

In a dual cable system providing 100 to 105 channels, both cables usually provide for upstream transmission in the 5 to 30 MHz range, thereby doubling the number of available upstream video, voice, and data channels.

Converters, addressable converters, and computer-controlled systems   Most cable systems built in the 1950s and 1960s had a capacity of 12 channels. These channels were transmitted downstream to subscribers on the same frequencies as the 12 channels that standard home TV sets are designed to receive.

With the advent of cable systems with higher transmission capacities, cable operators had to provide subscribers with devices called *converters* to enable them to receive the additional channels. Up to 24 channels could be accommodated by a converter often called an "A-B switch," providing the subscriber with two sets of 12 channels that could be tuned by a television receiver. To receive more than 24 channels requires increasingly sophisticated and costly converter technology.

Addressable converters, which are now being offered in many or most franchise bids in urban centers and metropolitan areas, represent a further advance in system sophistication. In a cable system with addressable converters, a computer at the system's headend controls the operation of the system and the delivery of services. The computer knows the electronic "address" of each subscriber and can deliver premium programming and other special services according to subscriber requests. Subscribers can add or drop premium services by pushing a button, and the cable operator can terminate services immediately for nonpayment of bills.

Addressable systems also make it possible to assemble audiences, one by one, for "pay-per-view" offerings such as college courses, sports, entertainment, and cultural events.

Interactive or "two-way" systems   Interactive or "two-way" systems are capable of two-way transmission—downstream from headend to subscriber, and upstream from subscriber to headend. Such transmission requires the installation of two-way amplifiers. Two-way amplifiers contain two amplifiers in each housing, one for transmission downstream and one for return signals originating at various points on the subscriber network and moving toward the headend.

One type of interactive transmission involves transmitting video from various sites in the community upstream to the headend. At the headend, these signals are converted to a higher frequency and retransmitted downstream to all subscribers.

Other types of interactive service allow each subscribing household to transmit a small amount of nonvisual electronic information back to the headend. This capability is involved in home burglar and fire alarm systems. When sensors in the home are activated, the information reaches the computer at the cable headend, which "knows" which home originated the signal.

Other services requiring upstream transmission capability from subscriber homes to the headend include polling, shopping, and banking at home, and access to computerized data and information—the "home information center."

Addressable converters are not necessarily interactive, however. They can permit computerized control of the reception of premium channels and pay-per-view material from the headend without providing any return transmission capability from the home. As with all increments in sophistication and capability, interactive addressable converters cost significantly more than one-way addressable converters. At this writing, addressable converters that can send nonvisual signals from each subscriber's home back to the headend cost about $250 each. Placing such devices in subscribers' homes is a major cost for cable operators.

Two-way addressable converters typically have a numeric keypad similar to that on a pocket calculator and several buttons for registering responses to opinion polls.

The numeric keypad is a satisfactory means for participating in interactive services such as banking and shopping at home and is probably good for accessing some forms of computerized data. It is less satisfactory, however, for accessing data in computerized data banks that have been set up to interface with home computers and other devices with alphanumeric keyboards. To some extent, a gap exists between the costliest device that cable systems can reasonably be expected to install in homes and the least costly way to access many forms of computerized data. The use of data banks, numeric keypad converters, and home computers is an area of cable technology that has barely begun to be explored at this writing.

1. One hertz (Hz) is a frequency of one cycle per second; one kilohertz (kHz) is one thousand hertz; one megahertz (MHz) is one million hertz; one gigahertz (GHz) is one billion hertz.

Telecommunications in the Year 2000

Joseph P. Martino

Telecommunications devices such as the telephone, radio, and television have brought about enormous changes in everyday life during the twentieth century. But even greater changes are in store for the 1980s and 1990s, thanks to developments now underway in communications technology.

Telecommunications, which is, essentially, the substituting of electrons for paper as the medium of communication, began in the 1850s with the invention of the telegraph. By 1870, the telegraph had captured 10% of all communications revenues in the United States. This transfer from paper to electrons continued with the introduction and spread, in the 1880s and 1890s, of the telephone. By 1900, telephone and telegraph between them accounted for 30% of all U.S. communications revenues. This fraction remained fairly level until the advent of radio, then started climbing again, reaching 45% in 1930.

During World War II, the fraction of U.S. communications revenues captured by telecommunications actually dropped, but bounded upward once more with the arrival of television. Sometime in the late 1950s, telecommunications first captured more than 50% of U.S. communications revenues. Currently, this fraction is over 60%, and, if the historical rate of substitution of electrons for paper is maintained, will reach 75% by the year 2000. Thus, in a century and a half, telecommunications will have risen in economic significance from zero to a commanding three-fourths of all expenditures for communications in the United States.

Reprinted with permission from the April 19, 1979, issue of *The Futurist*, published by the World Future Society, 4916 St. Elmo Avenue, Washington, D.C. 20014.

Broadcast television

One omnipresent segment of the telecommunications system is television. There are currently over 700 TV stations operating in the United States. Some 73 million black and white TV sets are currently in use, providing virtually 100% saturation of all U.S. households. There are also 54 million color TV sets in use, representing about 75% of all U.S. households. There are actually more U.S. households with TV than with toasters, electric coffee makers, or telephones. If present trends in commercial TV broadcasting continue, revenues to the industry by the year 2000 could go from their present level of roughly $4 billion a year to about $22 billion a year (in constant 1972 dollars). This would be enough to support 10 TV networks; however, there may not be that many networks.

The growth of cable television systems (CATV) and the spreading practice of independently producing programs for syndication rather than having them produced to order by networks may divert a significant fraction of future broadcast revenues away from networks to the individual producers and syndicating agencies.

Direct broadcast of TV programming from satellites is now technically feasible. If certain legal barriers are removed, satellite broadcasting might strengthen the networks but reduce or even eliminate local TV stations. If direct satellite broadcast does not come about, and historic growth continues, there should be 2,200 TV stations in the U.S. and large cities might have 15 or 20 different channels available by the year 2000.

The telephone system

The telephone system is almost as omnipresent as commercial TV. In 1977, there were 162 million telephones in the United States (compared with 257.5 million telephones in all other countries of the world combined!). Americans used the telephone to place an average of 467 million local calls and 38.8 million long-distance calls every day during 1977.

The growth of telephone use in the United States has had some interesting social implications. In 1936, the magazine *Literary Digest* incorrectly predicted the defeat of incumbent president Franklin D. Roosevelt based on a massive poll of persons whose names were obtained from telephone directories. In that year, telephone subscribers were not a representative cross-section of American voters: the wealthy were overrepresented and the poor underrepresented. That is hardly the case now, and by the year 2000, telephone subscribers will almost certainly comprise a fully representative cross-section of American voters—and consumers.

In terms of technology, there will be a significant shift away from the use of electrical wire for transmitting telephone signals in the years ahead, in favor of optical fibers. There will also be extensive transmission of data in digital form instead of analog form. This means that devices such as point-of-sale electronic funds transfer terminals, computer terminals, facsimile machines, etc., can be connected directly to the telephone line instead of requiring an acoustic coupler or other conversion device as is the case today. The telephone system will also be used extensively for automated (as opposed to manual or verbal) transfer of data for such purposes as check clearing, credit card verification, and order entry by salesmen or by customers ordering catalog items from suppliers. Communications satellites may have an important impact on long-distance telephone usage and rates in the future. Even today, satellite relays can provide less costly long-distance telephone links than terrestrial systems such as microwave connections.

Cable television

Cable television (CATV) is a rapidly growing segment of the telecommunications system. It originated as a means of providing television reception for communities in fringe areas distant from metropolitan centers with TV stations. It grew to become a means for providing significant alternatives to local broadcasting. Currently there are 14 million U.S. households with CATV, about 20% of the total. Typical CATV systems provide 10 to 20 channels, with programs from local and distant stations, as well as continuous weather data and other services.

By the year 2000, there should be 100 million households with CATV. There will be CATV systems in virtually every town over 2500 population—and in many rural areas as well. Few systems today have a return channel from the subscriber to the CATV "head end." But tomorrow's CATV systems, which will make extensive use of optical fibers in place of the wires and coaxial cables currently employed, will be able to offer two-way communication and even multi-way communication both between the subscriber and the "head end" and among individual subscribers.

Television programs from local and distant stations will still make up a significant fraction of CATV's offerings in the year 2000, but there will also be many additional services such as locally-focused public-service programs, educational courses, community debates, etc. In addition, there will be services that utilize "frame-grabbers" to continuously display a still picture on the TV screen. This will permit home viewers to receive directly printed material such as stock market reports, statistics, detailed news, etc. The return channel could be used to call up specific displays, which are then stored by the subscriber's frame-grabber until desired.

Telecommunications in the home

Telecommunications will invade the household in a variety of ways, some of them significantly different from the telephone, radio, and TV of today. TV games, for instance, are currently available in about 1 million U.S. households. This number should grow to 8 million by 1982, to 42 million by 1987, and to over 80 million by 1992. The games themselves will be much more sophisticated than those in use today, incorporating a built-in computer with the existing TV display.

One anticipated future development will be games played over cable television. These CATV games will utilize the two-way communications capability of future CATV systems to permit individuals to play against a computer at the CATV head-end or against human opponents elsewhere in the service area of the cable system. CATV games have already been introduced to subscribers of the QUBE two-way CATV system in Columbus, Ohio, and are expected to be available in 8 million homes by the late 1980s and in 50 million homes by the year 2000.

A significant advantage of these CATV games will be lower costs per user. Since the game "software" will be owned by the CATV system, each user can have access to a far greater variety of games than he would if he had to buy all of the software himself. In addition, the potential of playing against other human opponents in different households will make possible the organization of tournaments and similar activities.

Home video recorders that can record TV broadcasts and play them back through a TV set should become widely used before the end of the century. In addition, the growth of video-disc systems (offering easy playback and storage but no home recording capability) will permit the production and sale of specialized programs directly to consumers, bypassing the audience-size and ratings problems of the broadcast networks. For instance, opera-lovers and Shakespeare fans will be able to obtain videodiscs of their favorite performances, despite the fact that the market for such programs is small compared to the audience for a commercial network television program.

Videodiscs can store immense quantities of data and may someday replace printed books and reference works entirely. A videodisc playback device will be able to locate and display any recorded image and hold it on screen for as long as desired. Catalogs and encyclopedias on videodisc could combine passages of written material with animation, historical film footage, still photos, diagrams, or actual demonstrations and recorded experiments as illustrations. Instruction manuals for new appliances could show these devices actually being used. If videodiscs can be mass produced cheaply—for instance by offset printing on metal foil—and read by an inexpensive playback device, home-delivered videodiscs might even replace newspapers and magazines.

Another possible replacement for periodicals could be an updated version of the stock market ticker tape machine—a computer-controlled electronic printout device for the home or office. New books might be stored in a computer and printed out only on special order directly by the reader's home printer. Fast-breaking news items might be printed directly as received from wire service reporters on the scene. Such electronic media could be tailored to the specific interests of individual subscribers. Thus no two subscribers would receive exactly the same edition of the news. Instead, each would receive only those items or topics he considered most important, most interesting, or most relevant to his personal information needs.

Communications satellites

Communications satellites will grow in numbers and in the range of capabilities they provide to users. Currently there are about 20 commercial communications satellites in orbit. Their use is somewhat limited because of cost and regulatory problems. The number of possible communications satellites is limited by the amount of "parking space" available in orbit. If satellites are too close together, they will interfere with each other's signals.) Unless this problem can be overcome by future technological advances, the number and use of communications satellites will be severely limited. If these advances are made, the satellite channel capacity available to the United States in the year 2000 should be equivalent to 22,000 TV channels. To give some idea of how much communications capacity this represents, if every man, woman and child in the U.S. spent four hours a day transmitting messages on a teletype terminal, the resulting message traffic would just fill those 22,000 channels.

This additional communications capacity should make many new services possible. Telemedicine, involving satellite communications between ill or injured persons in remote areas and doctors in metropolitan areas, should be in wide use by the year 2000. Such a service could also aid accident victims by permitting nurses and medical aides on the scene or in the ambulance to administer emergency treatment under the direct supervision of a doctor located some distance away. Instrumented hospital beds may also become feasible, permitting patients in small or remote hospitals to be linked with computers or intensive-care monitors at some centralized location. Thus, even a small clinic, which could not justify the cost of building and staffing its own full-scale intensive care unit, could provide this emergency capability through a satellite communications link.

Disaster communications may also be conducted by satellite, since a portable satellite terminal could easily be moved into a disaster area, permitting communications even when existing systems such as telephone wires and radio stations had been knocked out.

Educational broadcasting via satellite will also be possible, providing televised lectures to persons in rural or remote areas. Continuing education courses, involving broadcasts to a limited number of students, with student feedback to the instructor during the class, will also be feasible. For practical reasons, most such classes would probably be limited to no more than 100 persons, but they could probably be offered at costs comparable to those of conventional continuing education courses today.

Public safety communications, such as those of police and fire departments, may well be sent via satellite, particularly since there are times when high sunspot activity will interfere with conventional ground-to-ground radio transmissions.

Another communications service that satellites might offer would be "remote testimony." Witnesses could testify at hearings held by government legislative or regulatory bodies without leaving their home towns. They would go to their local courthouse, be sworn in, and have their testimony televised via satellite to the state or national capital where the hearings were being held. This would provide a significant improvement in the democratic process by permitting the public at large easier access to state and federal legislators and regulatory agencies.

Special communications services

Many special services will also become available thanks to the widespread use of new developments in telecommunications. Some of these possible services include:

Electronic paychecks An employee's pay could be transmitted directly to his or her bank, without the need for handling paperwork of any kind.

Data base search Students, businessmen, scholars, and ordinary householders could make use of computerized data bases on a wide variety of subjects directly from home or office.

The information from these data bases might be printed out on a facsimile machine or simply displayed on a TV screen.

Computer conferencing   The ability to link participants at different locations to one another through a central computer could prove useful for both business and personal communication. Businessmen or government workers will be able to transmit messages, memos, and information among themselves wherever they happen to be. Private individuals might utilize this computer conferencing capability for such activities as "postal" chess matches, or to exchange information about hobbies or other topics of interest, as well as for planning joint participation in various activities.

Telecommuting   Much of the work of the modern office deals with the processing of information. For many employees, there is no real reason to be physically present at a central location, provided that they can have ready access to data banks and communication with other people. Typists, for instance, could work at or near their homes, receiving dictation by telephone or hand-written drafts by facsimile, and returning typed copy via "communicating" word-processing machines. Telecommuting could have a significant impact on the design of cities and on transportation requirements for the future. Some researchers believe that telecommuting is already economically competitive with conventional office practices; in the future, it will almost certainly be cheaper to "communicate to work" than to commute there.

The electronic library   Rather than visiting a library, any individual might be able to search the library files electronically and receive a printout of specific information or a facsimile copy of a desired document.

Mobile communications links   In the future, two-way radio facilities should be widely available in trains, trucks, taxicabs, etc. Whether this equipment will operate via satellite or will rely on an earth-based system will depend largely on the economic competitiveness of the two approaches. The technical feasibility of both is virtually certain. Businesses could keep close track of shipments moment by moment, even when the individual trucks are scattered across the country. Businessmen, government officials, and private individuals could keep in touch with their homes or offices continuously, despite being "on the move."

The growth of Citizen's Band (CB) radio usage in recent

years has been phenomenal. To many operators, CB serves as a means of escaping the limitations of the telephone. However, use of CB is inhibited by range restrictions and the limited number of channels available. The universal mobile communications service of the future would combine some of the advantages of CB with some of the advantages of the telephone. Portable hand-held units would permit subscribers to communicate with any other subscriber anywhere in the world, even while travelling.

Broadband switching   The ordinary telephone is a narrow-band communications system; that is, the range of frequencies that can be transmitted by telephone is much narrower than the range of sounds and signals that even a medium-quality stereo phonograph can handle. A broadband system is one that will transmit an extremely wide range of frequencies. CATV is an example of a broadband system. The typical TV cable system has the capability to transmit a dozen channels or more even now, and much greater carrying capacity will be possible in the future through the use of optical fibers.

A switched system is one in which any two subscribers can be connected directly together, like the telephone system. Most present-day CATV systems are not switched; signals can only be transmitted from the "head end" to the subscriber. A broadband switched system would combine the bandwidth of CATV with the switching capability of the telephone system. Among other things, a broadband switched network would make possible two-way video and high-speed data transmission between any two subscribers.

None of the developments I have outlined is inevitable. Some possibilities may not prove to be desirable; others may become realities in spite of widespread opposition. In many cases, whether certain services or capabilities develop will require decisive action to implement them and to remove barriers that might prevent their growth. Some of the important issues that have to be faced are discussed below.

Who will pay?

Commercial TV in the United States today is really a byproduct of advertising. The TV networks and stations hope to entice viewers to watch their offerings so that they can sell air time to advertisers. The individual viewer has little choice in programming, since economic considerations force networks and stations to aim for the largest possible audiences. There is no reason why TV has to be this way, however. "Pay TV" offers one possibility for giving the viewer greater control over programming. Presumably, if enough people are willing to pay for something, it will be offered. Nor is the limited number of available TV broadcasting frequencies a serious problem, since CATV can expand the number of channels almost indefinitely.

The dichotomy of "free TV" versus "pay TV" is really a false choice. We already pay for TV through the higher prices that manufacturers charge for their products when they pass along to the public the expenses they incur for TV advertising. Pay TV might give the American public the programming it wants at no greater cost than is being paid today. Existing legal constraints on pay TV would have to be removed, however, in order for this to happen.

Legislative action regarding TV advertising could also have a significant impact on the prospects for pay TV. Tobacco advertising is already banned from TV. Some groups are now urging that bans on TV advertising be imposed for other products, from alcohol and drugs to children's breakfast cereals. The elimination of any of these types of advertising might reduce the profitability of "free TV" and make "pay TV" more economically viable. In addition, growing pressure to ban certain types of programs as "undesirable" could create a market for such programs on videodisc or over "pay TV."

Will networks survive?

Commercial TV is today dominated by the networks. Again, this is not something that has to happen. Syndicated programs, produced independently of the networks and distributed to TV and CATV stations by their producers, provide a possible alternative. The relative growth of syndicated vs. network programming depends upon many political and regulatory decisions. The consequences of these decisions should be debated publicly before they are made, since the proper mix of syndication and network programming can give the public the best of both.

CATV has until quite recently been limited in its growth by governmental regulation, because of the threat it poses to network television. What this really meant was that the government and the networks felt the public would prefer CATV to broadcast TV, and to protect broadcast TV, the public was to be denied that choice. There have been some moves to unshackle CATV in the recent past. The public, however, should make its wants known to the regulatory agencies. Public interest, not protection of existing stations and networks, should be the principal consideration.

Direct broadcast TV from satellites promises to be cheaper than current systems and to provide more channels with a wider variety of programs. It is a direct threat, however, to existing stations. Here again a decision will be needed as to whether the interests of the public, or of the existing industry, will be served. Public debate on this issue is necessary. It should not be decided by those who have a vested interest in the current system.

Electronic mail is almost certain to occur, one way or another. An important decision, however, is whether it must be routed through the Post Office, or whether private organizations will be permitted to operate the electronic mail system. It is important to recognize that the historical justifications for governmental monopoly of the postal system no longer apply. The decisions regarding electronic mail should be made in the light of the best interests of the customers and users of the system, not in the interest of preserving an obsolete bureaucracy.

Monopoly or competition?

There are two possible technical bases for a broadband switched network. One is the CATV system, which will eventually reach most households. The other is the telephone system, once the wires and cables now in use are replaced by optical fibers. It might appear that an important issue is, which system should become the basis for the broadband switched network? However, that might be the wrong question. Perhaps it would be better to ask whether either should be precluded from providing broadband switched services?

There is no technical reason why both cannot provide such services to the same household. It is purely a question of economics whether one can succeed in driving the other out of business. If both were allowed to compete, both would probably survive, providing competing services and keeping costs down. Naturally, those in either of the industries would prefer to have their own industry given a monopoly on broadband services. The government would also prefer to see one system established as a monopoly, since then the government would have justification for regulating it. However, the consumer might well be better off if both telephone and CATV industries were allowed to compete for his business, with neither established as a monopoly and both free of regulation. Any decisions in this area should come only after a great deal of public debate, and a variety of experiments, to see what arrangements best serve the needs of the public.

As mentioned earlier, satellites are already cheaper than terrestrial systems for long-distance telephone calls. However, the telephone companies are continuing to build terrestrial systems, instead of moving extensively to satellite usage. There is a reason for this. Telephone companies are prohibited from owning satellites. Moreover, their rates are set to give them a "fair return" on their invested capital. If they build terrestrial facilities, those will be included in their "rate base" and the rates will be set to give a profit on them. If they lease satellite channels from the satellite owners, however, the lease payments are not part of their rate base, and they make no profit on them. They serve only as conduits for money from the subscriber to the satellite owner. Two sets of government regulations, each of which may apparently be justified by itself, combine to produce higher rates for long-distance calls. This is another issue that must be settled before the public can reap the full benefits of telecommunications technology. The issue should be settled on the basis of benefit to the public, not solely to serve the interests of the firms involved or of government regulatory agencies that justify their existence by denying benefits to the public, in the name of the good of that public.

The continued growth of telecommunications offers many worthwhile possibilities for great benefits to the public. However, these possibilities will not be realized automatically. In many cases the public will have to act to assure that they do become available, since many of them threaten existing services and industries, which will attempt to resist them. In particular, the public may have to overcome the tendency of regulatory agencies to freeze the telecommunications system into some historical pattern that is becoming obsolete because of technological change.

PART 2

Enhanced
Services

Cable Stakes Claim to Unmined Markets

Jeri Baker

The consumer side of the enhanced services issue is very much in the public eye. These are not luxury items like pay TV movies, after all. These are the long-heralded mass communications services—security, mail delivery, energy management, shopping and banking at home, and information retrieval. This high public awareness is due to publishers' involvement in the development of the business—as system buyers, as operators' joint venturers and as likely suppliers of data bases. To take only two dramatic examples, for Dow Jones and for the *New York Times*, the story of enhanced services is sprouting on their own bottom lines and it makes its way to line after line of widely disseminated print.

Publicity aside, however, just how much demand is there for extended services from cable hook-ups or, for that matter, from telephones? The most fundamental questions concern how to figure that demand, thus value, without getting differing answers. Cox and Sammons, Times Mirror and, of course, Warner Amex are spending lavishly to conduct on-site testing of new services. "Divide the expense of QUBE by the number of homes it won for Warner Amex in the franchise wars, and you have to conclude there isn't a company that wouldn't have paid for it gladly," says A.G. Becker analyst Tony Hoffman.

Not if you ask the companies. Sammons and Cox are at pains to point out that their pay-out will be "under $20 million" each, an obvious reference to the only number that Warner people will come close to acknowledging as the price tag for the

© 1981, Titsch Communications, Inc. All rights reserved. Reprinted from the June 1 issue of **CableVision**, with permission.

QUBE system. To ATC, "It isn't a matter of money. We have more than enough. It's how to spend it intelligently," says Executive Vice President for Corporate Development Michael McCrudden. It isn't necessary to swoop into a market with a handful of terminals. "That's technical, not consumer demand research." Unlike early pay TV, bedeviled by how to describe itself, the new services are so analogous to things people and providers already know that "you can get uncertainty down under 20 percent before you even go to the home with a sample." The obvious example to McCrudden: shopping. It is based on changing a small piece of an existing model—a printed catalog— for a TV screen. Ordering, fulfillment, processing, merchandising, direct-mail response rates are all known quantities.

To Times Mirror, actually offering a six-market shop-at-home service since April this year, it doesn't seem to have appeared that simple. "We had to start somewhere," shrugs business development chief John Cooke, describing the "undefined test phase." Driven by corporate electronic publishing issues, Times Mirror is also researching full-scale interactive videotex for early 1982 testing in a 200-home consumer trial in Orange County. The new staff, headed by corporate executive Jim Holly, is attached "for administrative purposes" to TM's cable wing, but will be neither a cable-only nor company-only offer. Of the initial volunteer homes, which will get the service free, half will be accessed via TM's local cable system and half via telephone lines. The test is slated to run nine months. Hardware and software now being developed has been purchased for "over $1 million" from Informart, owned by Southam Publishing and Torstar (part of *The Toronto Star*). Technology is Telidon. In addition to general information such as weather, sports and the like, the service will supply point-to-point electronic mail, messaging and shopping. It calls for on-line hookups to at least one bank for funds transfer and bill-paying. There will also be an on-line shopping service, which may be Comp-U-Card, the cable division's ally in its one-way shopping service. "We're not going to deliver signals in a video mode," says Holly, "but digital. We won't bother any other channel. And we'll make the cable system look like a telephone company."

The real key to a shopping service—and very likely to banking, with which it shares an essential characteristic—is how will people react to the loss of check and credit card float? The impact of genuine two-way transactions which TM is moving toward in retailing and banking will be uncomfortably immediate. Teleprompter's power load management experiment in Grosse Pointe could face a similar human drawback, no matter how well it tests in the abstract: can consumers be persuaded that there is any personal benefit to permitting a gas or electric company to shut off air conditioners or water heaters at its discretion? Teleprompter exults in the development of a low cost modem to handle its meter-reading service because the Datavision product's intelligence is "expandable" to other services. It looks to de-bundling security elements connectable to the modem, for example. "Who in their right mind would turn down fire and burglary protection?" asks Corporate Development Vice President Andrew Goldman, sharing the now well-accepted conviction that security is the easiest of enhanced services to add. But the power-related offers are services to be sold to utility companies themselves, not consumers. It is the utilities, then, who pay for the modem, letting the operator add other uses for it with more speed than if he had to cover the expense on subscriber revenue. And the marketing to businesses—doubtless eager to stop sending out meter readers—neatly sidesteps that awkward approach to consumers about giving up control of their home environments.

Inherent in all the consumer-persuasion problems, of course, is time. The success of at-home services for which there is no ready equivalence test like the price of theater tickets versus pay TV is dependent on buyer education. As marketers used to say about dual pay channel offers, "It doesn't pay to be first." Those sticking determinedly to a position "behind the power curve" (as eager product suppliers would have it), are not at all apologetic about watching to see what happens before making the investment in plant that enhanced services of any scope demand.

The widow and orphans?

There are those who use those same cost considerations as an astringent cooler to overheated fears of AT&T. The "onesy-twosy" orders from telcos for the latest in fiber optic technology are just what they sound like: proof of testing the two-way information services beyond voice transmission, which will lead to the confrontation with cable providers. But the reason they test, say observers, is because they must find new services themselves to fund the new optical plant they require for their main business. Cable's basic-plus-pay revenue helps withstand plant costs. Data transmission could be added as an incremental service without the burden of contributing enormous amounts to cash flow. Telcos haven't the same base. With huge investments in still-unamortized plant, their necessarily aggressive move toward data services would leave staggering depreciation and amortization costs in its wake. But if the move isn't made, it will soon be cheaper to lease channel space from cable than to over-build the enhanced services system if cable wins the footrace.

"The perception of AT&T might is such that we board up

the windows when they ride into town," says Bob Schmidt, whose Communications Technology Management hopes to spearhead cable's move to information services. To that, the view of analyst Tony Hoffman is tonic: "AT&T simply cannot decide to lose money for a while. To dilute earnings while it builds a new data business is against its whole structure, financing, rate-setting—all designed for steady payment of dividends to shareholders. The chairman who bucks that would be lynched."

What AT&T proposes to do about built-in limits comes clearer in this look at its struggle for deregulation and what prompted it.

AT&T in the maelstrom

Major pieces of telecommunications deregulation dovetailed around year end. More aptly, they collided and their impact may direct the development of cable services to come.

In late 1980 the Federal Communications Commission decided it would not regulate what it defined as enhanced services—anything computer-processed and providing more than plain transmission of information. It could regulate them, it says, but it won't. While such services are beyond the scope of its jurisdiction over interstate communications of common carriers, it could get at them by assertion of ancillary jurisdiction, that broad designation which gave it authority over cable television in the first place.

If the decision stands up under appeal, "Computer II" (product of the Second Computer Inquiry) cuts a clear swath for cable to enter the two-way interactive business. But it does very much the same thing for AT&T, and it is well to remember that was the point of the action. Since 1956, AT&T has been barred by consent decree from providing more than rate-regulated common carrier communication service. The FCC would let an unregulated new subsidiary leap the bar. Telcos would still be unable to have any ownership interest in cable anywhere they provide telephone service as well. (That restriction, adopted partly to give cable a chance to develop broadband services, also shows signs of melting.) The immediate effect is to chart telcos and cable systems on a converging path.

The other deregulatory flame under enhanced services is the competitive carrier rulemaking. Last November, in its First Report and Order on the subject, the FCC proposed to free "non-dominant" specialized common carriers from rules on tariffs and authorization of new services. Reasonably enough, it had decided they just lacked the market clout that would let them be abusive even if there were no watchdog. In January [1981], the commission issued a Further Notice of Proposed

Rulemaking, an open-handed removal of the label "common carrier." Only AT&T and Western Union would stay corraled, because they alone could dominate in free-for-all negotiations with leases.

As customers of terrestrial domestic satellite and miscellaneous common carriers, cable operators could be adversely affected. Vendors of video transmission service would no longer have to greet any qualified use with nondiscriminatory, cost-based rates. Microwave and satellite fees would rise, priced according to demand. But the commission figures that would spur new entrants to the transponder-supply business, pushing prices down in the longer term.

At the same time, however, the move might be an asset to cable systems, letting them lease channels themselves without triggering the fearsome common carrier designation. As private carriers, they would not be serving all comers. They could lease channels under individual contracts to interstate communications services in need of local distribution loops.

The commission clearly intends to try to block local regulators from stepping into the breach it leaves behind it. It does have the authority to preempt intrastate governance at odds with federal policy aimed at interstate deregulation.

But what if that is not what happens? What if the state does move in putting what might have been deemed competitive common carrier services under public utility regulation? In a move that dismayed many, Manhattan Cable decided the better part of valor would be to file with the public service commission when it began to move from an experiment in two-way data transmission to a full-fledged business.

In 1974, when it introduced bank-to-bank, computer center-to-computer center data service, it promptly heard from the PSC. In its show cause order, the commission challenged MCTV's right to engage in a business traditionally offered by telephone companies without subjecting itself to the same PSC authority telcos are under. The filing was supported by New York Telephone and opposed by the city, the state cable commission and Manhattan Cable. There has never been a decision.

Hanging fire

Cable's full plunge into computer-driven enhancements and real two-way interactivity is inextricably linked to the swirl around AT&T's plan to expand voice carriage to data, text and video.

Ma Bell, however, has been taking a studiously peaceable tack. Though the lunge for a piece of the information market "bigger than all telephony as we once conceived it," as AT&T chairman Charles Brown described it to shareholders, certainly goes on, it is presented now in two ways: Vice Chairman James

Olson's espousal of what is clearly intended to be winning candor and reasonableness before the American Newspaper Publishers Association and residence Marketing Vice President Dennis Sullivan's mission to court the cable industry begun at an NCTA executive seminar on enhanced services. Requesting an end to "bare knuckles boxing matches," Olson asked the publishers to consider that for every AT&T move into electronics, there are competitors, with cable itself "the fastest growing alternative communications network." If AT&T is permitted to add information services to its transmission and equipment base, "the world will not come to an end." The company has not argued about the essence of its deregulation—the creation of a separate subsidiary—and Olson says it is "prepared to accept reasonable legislative and regulatory constraints which will insure against cross-subsidy [from its business and residential service], and provide safeguards against even the appearance of unfair competition." What it doesn't want—and Olson asked his listeners to acknowledge the wrongness of it—is legislation (or lobbying) that would "foreclose our business from applying its own technology to its own business."

Sullivan's task is to come up with specific disarming tactics. "AT&T has no intention of going into cable's retransmission or program origination business. There's so much contention about our converging courses, when what is really happening is opportunity for synergism." What is on Sullivan's mind is a hybrid, an alternative "to thousands of non-interconnected systems having to spend big money to go two-way. The telephone line from the home has more capability than interactive cable. Cable's topology is a high-speed highway to the home. Getting back from the home is another matter. Look at shopping via cable. Nice high-resolution pictures, yes. But the store doesn't happen to be at the headend. Through our switched lines, we can carry a message anywhere."

It would take some design work, of course, Sullivan says. Thousands of attempts to place orders through the telco central office would make for nightmarish congestion. But, MSOs at various stages of circumventing phone lines do face much larger problems. Times Mirror's six-market shop-at-home offer uses an 800-telephone number for upstream communication. But its plans for a system-wide-and-beyond version of shopping, banking, metering and electronic mail will be two-way cable all the way. "We're talking about a fully digital system, interconnected data bases, computers talking to computers," says TM executive Jim Holly. "It's very tricky stuff. We're getting there, but there's much more engineering work to be done." The Sammons-Dow Jones venture outside Dallas is equally complex. After it had been selling its two-way information retrieval service for six months, acceptance was "not as good as we'd like," says Information Vice President Jerry Caddy. Sammons is acting as distributor for Apple, Atari and Texas Instruments home terminals to get the market off the ground. But, that's a business it doesn't really want to be in: it's an expensive proposition to consider distribution in the thousands, so only about 50 have been put out. Subscribers can lease them for $20-$80 monthly for two or three months as a pre-buy test. Hobbyists, who would have their own terminals—and are, along with professionals, the group the terminal manufacturers rely on—are not prospects for the data bases Dow Jones supplies. They prefer to write their own programs. Casual users face another problem: while the Dow Jones material has been revamped entirely for the cable consumer, other data banks are inappropriate for easy home use.

(If all cable customers were between the ages of seven and ten, cable's move into all enhanced services would be considerably eased. On a significant level, the problem of expansion into banking, shopping, viewdata and the like is not the telephone industry, not the thorny questions of whether to provide channels or joint venture or enter new businesses independently. The problem is that the gadgetry new services will need is "non-friendly," as the term of art puts it—unless the user is a curious kid. "It has to be as easy to use as the telephone," says Warner Amex's business development chief, Bob Sullivan, in what many will find a haunting analogy. "You have to have a prompting situation—press a button and it's there," agrees Caddy.)

Sammons' system sets great store by storage—the ability to call up information and manipulate it—disdaining the telephone industry's (and cable competitor's) dial-it services which simply "spew information across the screen." But that takes a smart terminal—one with a memory. Some users have them, some don't. And that lack of standardization is a problem all around. How, for instance, are all bases to be friendly to all terminals when characters-per-line, lines-per-screen, differ?

The weakest link is still the modems, the "HIT" or "home interface terminals" that translate between the home link and the system. By most accounts, they are paste-up, temporizing versions of a real cable-ready device. The Electronics Industries Association is working toward standards, but with none in hand, parallel developments are headed for a clash, especially if proprietary users such as Sammons, whose HIT was made to order to TOCOM, decide to market to the rest of the industry.

Whether entertainment channels on cable are eclipsed by shopping, banking and all the varieties of computer-allied services, whether consumer service is itself secondary to voice/data transmission for giant companies linked by orbiting computers is a question that ought to be answered within five years.

Getting Ready for Videotex, Teletext and the Interactive Worlds Beyond

Gary Arlen

Videotex and teletext epitomize the progress of the cable television industry. Eighteen months ago, only a handful of visionaries knew the terms; now the services are ingrained within every major cable franchise proposal. To be sure, the concept which videotex and teletext represent—interactive cable—has been on industry lips for more than a decade. But only in the past few years has everyone gotten specific, settling down with names and specific services which can be offered by the technologies.

This is not to say, of course, that the issues are resolved, not by any means. The videotex/teletext business is still loaded with questions. There is immense confusion about which direction these businesses should go. That leads to false starts, backtracking, front-stabbing and a constant eye on what is going on in other corners of the videotex arena. ("Front-stabbing" is a growing trend we've noticed in which rival technocrats, e.g., British, French, Canadian, openly criticize the quality and capabilities of each others' facilities.)

Unexpected bonanza

The spurt of videotex and teletext activity can be attributed to a number of simultaneous developments. First and foremost is the economic appeal. Several independent research projects—all surfacing in the past year—have forecast an extraordinary bonanza in the information and transactional services marketplace, perhaps as much as $3 billion annually by mid-decade. This figure includes prospective advertising and information

© 1981, Titsch Communications, Inc. All rights reserved. Reprinted from the June 1 issue of **CableVision**, with permission.

provider revenues, equipment purchases and facilities income. That jackpot would be split several ways: between telephone, cable and broadcast companies, information and service providers. But, in any case, it's an attractive supplement to the other on-line information services which are growing in the professional marketplace.

From a strategic planning position, videotex and teletext are seen as important ancillary services which fulfill a number of social and educational needs. They are relatively inexpensive add-ons, which can be piggybacked to current communications services. They are useful in a society which is becoming even more geared to at-home activities thanks to such factors as working wives, high gasoline prices and other situations which make it efficient to telecommunicate. Moreover, the "information age" has presumably created a thirst for easier access to more types of data, be it sports scores or scientific research. Teletext and videotex permit easier access to such databases.

In addition, the promotional push by British, French, and Canadian technocrats has accelerated interest in videotex and teletext. All three countries are eager to sell their technologies in the U.S., which is regarded as the primary information market. At the same time, on-going research within the telephone and broadcasting industries has come up with systems which are ready to be merchandized. Coincidentally, the foreign incursion jibes with U.S. research, therefore fueling the push to develop and market interactive technologies.

Thanks to this combination of stimuli, videotex and teletext technologies are speeding ahead at an increasingly rapid rate. Moreover, other developments—such as the Computer Inquiry II decision—have opened the door for AT&T to enter the business, which it fully intends to do, thus contributing additional technology plus marketing and legal headaches.

The state of videotex art itself has also increased dramatically during the past few years. The original block letters and rudimentary graphics have given way to stylized, highly detailed graphics—even full-color photos which can be built up on the screen using only a fraction of the bandwidth needed for full-frame video.

Indeed, the technology's ability to deliver such services contributes to the lively competition between cable and telephone company proposals. Thanks to new facilities, a small telephone wire can deliver many of the same services as interactive cable—albeit current telephone facilities fall far short of being able to offer most of the other broadband services which cable can provide. To the end-user, however, the broadband capability may become less important—replaced by more significant features such as switched services and low priced terminals of the telephone version.

Cable's pivotal position

Cable's traditional one-way service plus its emerging interactive capacity creates a situation in which the industry has a foot in each camp: teletext and videotex. Thanks to its multi-channel capability, cable can enhance teletext signals, providing extra outlets for data transmitted via the vertical interval. That, in essence, is the idea behind SSS's Cable Text and other satellite-fed teletext services in which a single band of video results in several channels of video image at the user's terminal. Simultaneously, cable can also provide many broadband interactive services—potentially with much better services than can telephone lines.

This combination of capabilities places cable in a pivotal role. In cases where limited interaction is needed, cable is an ideal medium. At the same time, the two-way capacity leads to substantial new options for tele-shopping, tele-banking and other interactive services.

However, there are also several shortcomings on cable's side. As competitors avidly point out, only about half of America's homes will be wired for cable within the decade—and, of that number only a fraction (perhaps under 10 percent of all U.S. homes) will have two-way cable facilities. This limitation could diminish cable's role as a provider of interactive services, but it won't eliminate cable's multi-channel capacity for teletext-type services.

Moreover, cable's broadband capacity can be easily married with telephone circuits for up-stream interaction. That's part of the concept behind the recently announced Inteltext system, developed by French technologists. The technology would permit viewers to call up specific data via a telephone line; that information would then be down-loaded to a caller's terminal using the full bandwidth of the cable if necessary. Data could be delivered on demand (within a matter of seconds, as on a conventional teletext system), or it could be ordered for delivery at a later time—an attractive feature if the user wants a sizeable batch of information.

Such hybrid formats are likely to become a mainstay of the new technology. KSL, the Booneville Broadcasting station in Salt Lake City, has already experimented with a similar "Two Way Teletext" system, using a phone line for call-up of specific pages. As the enthusiasm over teletext and videotex continues to grow, analysts expect more such variations to surface.

In addition, cable's plunge into videotex/teletext service for the traditional consumer audience comes at the same time that many industry leaders are beginning to romance business users. Simultaneously, major companies are beginning to take seriously cable's potential for broadband delivery of services within a metropolitan area; thanks to new plans for regional interconnection and satellite hops, cable is at last becoming viable as a carrier of high-speed, high-capacity data transmission.

Questions galore

This dynamic state of affairs has led to a proliferation of questions: serious, fundamental issues which are just now being raised. Each question may have several answers, meaning that it could take years to hammer out realistic solutions to basic issues which will guide the development of videotex and teletext.

Standards   Even as a debate smolders as to whether the U.S. should adopt technical standards for teletext, British, French and Canadian interests have submitted proposals for specific technical guidelines. The most optimistic observers agree it will take one to two years for such standards to be hammered out, during which time unregulated videotex formats will be installed and in operation.

Format   Oak Communications is actively working on at least two and maybe more, different videotex formats. Oak has developed a technology for Cox Cable's current INDAX project, but it is also working up its own decoder for other cable videotex trials. In addition, Oak has at least two different over-the-air pay teletext projects in mind, one of which has already been tested on Oak's Florida STV station using an aural subcarrier instead of the traditional vertical blanking interval.

Field trials   Time Inc., expected to become a leader in the industry because of its database strengths (literally millions of morsels from its decades of publishing magazines and newspapers), appears to be hedging its bets. It is launching a highly publicized satellite-fed teletext test using an HBO transponder and one of its cable TV systems (apparently ATC's Albany, New York, operation). But, in addition, Time will also test teletext on a smaller scale, via a locally generated trial on its Orlando, Florida, ATC system.

Competition   Times-Mirror Corporation will do a full-scale videotex trial in its southern California region, using both cable and telephone technology. On the surface it sounds like a valid comparative process, using different delivery systems to test consumer usage of the same or similar databases.

Legal   Perhaps the touchiest of areas, legal and regulatory questions about videotex and teletext are just starting to be asked. Answers appear to be years away. In the teletext realm, the most timely matter is the legal skirmish between WGN Continental Broadcasting and United Video, a confrontation over who owns the vertical blanking interval. In the overall world of electronic information and transactional services, there will be immense battles over privacy, access, operations and all the other matters which keep lawyers busy.

Consumer appetite   Tocom, which included a "text" feature in its 55-Plus equipment introduced at last year's NCTA convention, had to pull back within six months. It found that a textless decoder (priced about $50 less) was more attractive to cable operators, and presumably their customers. If nothing else, the incident underscores the problem of consumer education: viewers have to become familiarized with the concept of electronic information and services. Right now, families understand how to watch TV for entertainment and information video programming. The leap into interactive information retrieval and tele-marketing takes a separate form of media savvy, which could be a generation away.

Bell's role   AT&T is, undoubtedly, the major factor in the videotex and teletext business in the U.S. today—even though it is just now hinting at some of its plans for the industry. Its market clout could mean that its choice of a videotex technical standard will *de facto* become the U.S. format, if only because most analysts believe that the videotex standard should be compatible with over-the-air transmission and reception technologies. Newspapers have already loudly (and fairly successfully) lobbied against AT&T's entry into the information business—a fight in which they are joined by computer and data processing firms, the cable industry and other substantial foes. Many—but significantly, not all—of the nation's leading publishers are waging an attack to keep AT&T out of the videotex software business, especially fearing that Bell's concept may bite deeply into classified advertising, which represents as much as 65 percent of a newspaper's ad revenues.

What's popular   "Software is the name of the game." It's becoming a familiar line in the cable and new video environment, and nowhere is it more true than in teletext and videotex. The database—the actual information which users can look up—is at the heart of the service. That's why promoters envision teletext as primarily a news and information service, with timely and pertinent material such as news headlines, sports, weather and stock market reports that can be reached at any time. In fact, Ceefax (the BBC's teletext service, which has been in operation for several years) finds that news headlines, an electronic TV guide (listings of tonight's TV programs) and a fun and games package (riddles, quizzes and simple videogames) are the most popular pages, i.e., the most-often accessed.

MDS, LPTV and STV

Of course, "established" media such as cable, telephone and commercial TV are not alone in their quest for videotex and teletext opportunities. Purveyors (and prospective operators) of multipoint distribution service, subscription TV and—significantly—low power television are hungry to get into the teletext business. For example, among the LPTV applications are impressive ones such as those from the newly created communications subsidiary of Federal Express, the air freight company. Like several other applicants, Federal Express proposes full channel teletext service during daytime—probably for business data, freight information and other professional transmissions. At night, the channel would be used for pay TV.

Existing pay TV companies are already on the teletext trail—notably Oak Communications, which completed a text experiment on its Ft. Lauderdale STV channel. The prospects of "pay teletext," handled via the existing STV decoder, is encouraging Oak to try another test (using a different technology) on its Los Angeles STV channel. Meanwhile, the company that operates SelecTV has also developed a number of facilities for transmitting data as well as multiple audio channels.

In addition, several MDS companies are already deeply involved in teletext projects. STAR, the Richmond, Virginia-based MDS company, began inserting teletext information into its vertical blanking interval a year ago, using an Apple computer to create text pages of local information. On a larger scale, Microband, the MDS industry giant, is working with Tymshare (the company which bought it last year) to develop local data transmission services.

The video vending machine

Videotex is a business where the dessert is served before the meat and potatoes. First timers using the technology generally fall in love with the pleasant novelties of instant information, videogames and similar delights. But after the gimmickry wears off, videotex gets down to the serious business which promises to become the mainstay of interactive technology: tele-shopping, tele-banking and other services which will become the foundation of the new technologies.

Cable is not ignoring those opportunities and is hard at work on finding the best way into that field. Cox Cable appears to be furthest along right now with its INDAX system, ready for start-up in San Diego, Omaha and New Orleans. Source Telecomputing will supply the information database, and Cox has signed up two newly created subsidiaries of American Can Company to handle the tele-marketing package. HomeServ (a small company which made its debut at 1980's NCTA convention and was subsequently acquired by American Can) is coordinating the activities of about a dozen banks, S&Ls and financial institutions for the test. Another newly created ACC arm, Interactive Marketing Services (a new division of Fingerhut direct mail giant) will handle tele-marketing via its "ViewMart" service.

Of course, such services are still rudimentary—just as the tele-merchandising ventures available via the on-going Viewtron experiment in Coral Gables, Florida, a joint venture of AT&T and Knight-Ridder Newspapers. In a somewhat different vein, Times-Mirror Cable is aloft with its "Shopping Channel" service, a full-video marketing channel, with purchases conducted via Comp-U-Card's phone-in ordering service.

All these services and several others underway (including one to be managed by Communications Technology Management) underscore the eagerness afoot within the cable industry and other communications groups to find a route into the lucrative electronic mall of tele-marketing.

For those late comers

Videotex and teletext are look-alike technologies which marry computers and television—opening vast possibilities for information retrieval and other electronic services. Videotex (sometimes called "viewdata") is the hardwire, two-way format: telephone or cable lines connect the main database computer with the end user. In comparison, teletext is a one-way broadcast service, with data beamed to users' homes encoded within the TV signal.

In both cases, the user calls up specific "pages" of information via a terminal about the size of a handheld calculator. A videotape receiver can be incorporated within a home computer, thus promising access to massive databases and interaction.

Videotex and teletext pages appear in the form of computer

read-outs, often with computer graphics to illustrate the image. Originally the graphics were straightforward, block-like images, and that style is still the foundation of the "alpha-geometric" formats, such as the British and French systems. However, both of those systems now also allow for higher-grade, more neatly defined drawings and still pictures in the alpha-geometric and alpha-photographic styles.

In addition to information retrieval, videotex offers a form of time-sharing which is the gateway to comprehensive two-way services, such as tele-shopping and tele-banking.

Teletext is traditionally encoded on lines of the vertical blanking interval (that thick black stripe you see when a TV picture rolls over). In recent proposals, however (especially for low-power TV and new MDS channels), there are plans to devote the entire channel capacity for teletext-type data transmission—thus increasing the system capacity and speed.

Teletext pages can be called up when a TV set is tuned to a channel transmitting data in the vertical interval. Data is constantly cycled through along with each video field. By pushing a button on the decoder, the viewer can see the text pages instead of the video image; another button permits text pages to be superimposed over a standard video picture. The superimposing feature opens the door for "closed captioning" and other program related teletext service. (However, the current closed captioning service offered by ABC, NBC and PBS via Sears' Tele-Caption decoders operates on "Line 21" of the vertical interval, rather than the traditional lines 15-16 now planned for teletext use.)

Among the most important differences between videotex and teletext is the system's capacity. Typical users of these services want the information within five to ten seconds after they push the buttons to call up a page. A longer lag makes them lose interest. That limitation means that teletext can only provide a maximum of about 800 pages—and probably closer to 400 pages—of data per channel. In comparison, the interactive videotex systems can handle a vast number of pages—whatever the computer storage banks can hold. For example, the British Prestel videotex system now holds about 200,000 pages.

Basically, videotex information can be divided into two categories: library data, such as research information which doesn't have to be updated often or ever (for example a list of U.S. presidents) and replenishable data, or items that need frequent revision, such as the latest voting returns on election day.

The trial trial

For several years, international communicators have been trekking along an ever-lengthening trail, leading them from city to city, country to country on the lookout for new developments in videotex and teletext service. Broadcasters, cable and telephone companies have been involved in one or another experiment—all of which have been closely watched, but few of which have had substantial outputs of tangible results.

In Europe and the Far East, exotic tests of tele-shopping, electronic classifieds ads and other services are underway. In Columbus, Ohio, OCLC, a major educational library research firm, conducted a much-publicized information retrieval test of database access. (Because of its location, the OCLC test, which used telephone lines and a microcomputer at each home, was often confused with QUBE.) And in London, actual full-time operating services have been available for several years: Prestel Viewdata, Ceefax and Oracle teletext.

Now the pace of testing is picking up: teletext trials have begun in Washington, Chicago, and Los Angeles. AT&T's Electronic Information Service II in Austin, Texas (currently under court review after the newspaper industry challenged it), is supposed to offer electronic classified advertising in addition to other electronic phone directory services. PlayCable—which offers many of the services of a basic videotex system in addition to its videogame capacity—has completed market trials in five cities and is due for nationwide marketing.

Experts have also tried to draw conclusions from QUBE in Columbus, although that system is far from the sophisticated retrieval service now envisioned by videotex planners.

This proliferation of trials has turned up a few valuable results, but in many ways, the multitude of experiments has muddied the waters, offering bits and pieces of data—but rarely coming to concrete conclusions. For example, many of the tests have been done without charging users for the service. That's invalid if the eventual systems do assess monthly subscription fees or per-access charges. Moreover, the continued testing has encouraged many prospective participants to stand by, let others assume the experimental costs, then plunge in after a body of knowledge has been established for running the actual service.

What happens next appears to be anybody's guess. If "one-upmanship" has become standard operating procedure within the cable industry at large, it is a natural state of affairs within the videotex/teletext fraternity. Anything the French can do, the British can do better. And the Canadians can do better still. And AT&T may be able to leapfrog all of them . . . until somebody else has a better idea.

It creates a lively new business—and one which the cable TV industry is intent upon exploiting.

Enhanced and Interactive Services

Janet Quigley

A modern cable system can provide many kinds of electronic services to the home in addition to standard television. Not long ago these services were collectively referred to as cable's "blue sky." Now they are being routinely offered in cable franchises in urban centers and metropolitan areas. Such services include the following:

1. Home security and fire alarms
2. Shopping and banking at home
3. Polling
4. Pay-per-view programming
5. Video and instructional games
6. Meter reading and energy management
7. Home information services, including teletext, videotex, and access to data banks and computerized sources of information.

As of this writing, a few systems have had experience with security and fire alarm service on cable, (this topic is discussed in another article). Market experience has been limited with the other services discussed in this article. Thus, an adequate profile of their relative commercial prospects has not yet emerged.

In some instances, such services require or work most efficiently with home computers as terminals rather than with the numeric keypad usually associated with two-way address-able cable converters. Such computers, of course, are proliferating rapidly in American homes.

Reprinted with permission from *The Community Medium*, volume 1 of *CTIC Cablebooks*, edited by Nancy Jesuale with Ralph Lee Smith (Arlington, Va.: Cable Television Information Center, 1982).

Cable, however, is not required as the communications link for home computer access to various databases, services, and information. In most instances, access is made through the telephone system. Cable's ultimate role as a link to these sources of information has not been fully established.

To help make cable more attractive as a delivery medium, "packages" of various types of enhanced and interactive services are being created, including some services available only through the cable system and services that a computer owner might access separately.

A short discussion of the status of each major type of service is provided in the following text. This is followed by descriptions of QUBE and INDAX, two commercial "packages" for cable subscribers in which several interactive services and capabilities are combined and tailored for cable subscriber use.

Home shopping

Pilot programs for home shopping services by cable were introduced in 1981 by Cox, Times Mirror, Adams-Russell, Modern Satellite Network, and the Great American Teleshopping Network. CompuServe, available on Warner-Amex's Columbus system, includes classified ads from newspapers it carries. These services use both one- and two-way technology.

A two-way service, Comp-U-Star, provides discount shop-at-home services to owners of home computers. Comp-U-Star is a data retrieval system. It lists products using alphanumeric displays. As of January 1982, the firm offered more than 30,000 products, the descriptions of which are entered into the database in a way that permits comparison shopping. It lists all items of a given type by price, brand name, and other categories. "Shopping" can be done at any hour, and goods are delivered to the subscriber's home. Purchases are charged to the major credit card designated by the user. The subscriber receives a personal membership number and password, which must be entered to make transactions. Membership costs $25 per year; the member also pays connect time charges of 50 cents per minute from 9 a.m. to 5 p.m. on weekdays and 25 cents per minute at other times. Times Mirror has been testing Comp-U-Star on cable, and the firm is seeking other cable affiliations.

Times Mirror is testing a one-way shopping service with Sears, Roebuck and Co. The Sears service is a television program that displays and describes merchandise; viewers make purchases by pressing buttons on an addressable converter or other type of interactive terminal. There is some speculation that visual images might encourage impulse buying more than alphanumeric displays would, but consumer acceptance of either the Sears or the Comp-U-Star approach has not been established.

The Modern Satellite Network has carried the "Home Shopping Show" since 1980. The talk-show format allows retailers to discuss and demonstrate a product or line of products in a "soft-sell" approach termed an "infomercial." Products are not directly marketed during the show, but some retailers experiment with cable audience interest by offering discount coupons or "giveaways" via a toll-free number. Retailers pay $11,000 for an 8½-minute interview or $29,000 for a full half-hour.

Cox is currently testing a shopping feature as part of INDAX, its information retrieval service. The subscriber chooses a product from the INDAX data bank and orders it via an addressable converter. The order is registered in the INDAX computer and transferred to an "electronic middleman," Viewmart, which handles all contacts with retailers. Viewmart processes the order and bills purchases to the credit card number provided by the subscriber.

Home banking

Home banking is more complex than home shopping. It requires arrangements with banks, provisions for security, and the appropriate hardware and software to perform several functions. Subscribers should be able to obtain bank balances, make transfers, and pay bills. Bank Ohio in Columbus, Ohio, has tested such a service through a combination of cable and telephone lines.

Times Mirror is planning a 6-month home-banking experiment with Bank of America in San Diego. Users will be able to pay utility bills by cable as well as determine balances and make transfers.

In Cox's Mission system, also in San Diego, banking is being coordinated by HomServ, another "interactive middleman." HomServ handles all negotiations with banks and retail merchants to authorize credit card and bank account transactions. The main components of the Cox/HomServ system are account inquiry, bill payments, and direct ordering of retail merchandise. Airline reservations and home security can be incorporated into the system.

Polling

Two-way addressable converters with numeric keypads permit viewers to transmit a limited selection of responses back to the headend in response to queries or requests for information made on the screen. The responses of viewers are instantly compiled by a computer at the headend, and the tabulations are shown immediately on the screen.

In the QUBE system in Columbus, Ohio, the system's polling capability has often been used for entertainment purposes. By indicating their preference among five different response options presented to them on the screen, subscribers have voted on magazine covers, the merits of amateur performers, the round-by-round progress of prize-fights, desired endings for soap operas, and choice of plays in football games. Other applications are informational, such as consumer information programs in which viewers signal their reactions to various products and services.

More important questions are raised by the use of cable's polling capabilities in political matters. QUBE viewers have been asked to provide their opinions on political issues and events, to react to political speeches and debates as soon as they appear on the screen, and to express opinions on the outcome of forthcoming elections. Some analysts believe that widespread use of such instantaneous and unrepresentative but highly visible material may have an adverse effect on the political decision-making process by obscuring, distorting, underrepresenting, or oversimplifying the true opinions of the public.

Pay-per-view

In a computer-controlled, addressable cable system, the computer knows the electronic "address" of each subscriber. This capability is used to respond to subscriber requests for various premium programming. The computer can immediately activate the premium channel or channels that the subscriber requests. It can also be used to disconnect service when a subscriber has stopped a service or has not paid bills promptly.

This capability also makes it possible to assemble audiences, subscriber by subscriber, for individual programs that such subscribers are willing to pay for. Such offerings can include professional sports events, first-run movies, popular music concerts, and other types of entertainment; cultural material; college credit courses; and computer-assisted instruction.

As the cable industry grows, so does its bidding power in the programming marketplace. The medium's attractiveness to professional sports and entertainment promoters may increasingly take the form of selling such material on a pay-per-view basis. This development could have an adverse impact on the current structure of over-the-air broadcasting, and important commercial and political battles could ensue. The development of pay-per-view for individual entertainment and sports events on cable could be hastened by the growth of subscription television (over-the-air pay TV), which could be a joint bidder with cable for various top-rated events.

For local groups, pay-per-view offers the possibility of transmitting special programs and events from local civic and community centers, thereby providing a greater basis of financial support for such events. In education, pay-per-view opens up possibilities for transmission of course material directly to the home.

Interactive capability is not required for pay-per-view service—subscribers can "order programming" by placing a phone call or mailing a postcard to the cable company. In the current developmental state of pay-per-view programming, subscribers on systems where it is offered must often phone or mail in their requests days or weeks prior to the showing of the program. In the future, it is anticipated that addressable converters that enable subscribers to "order" individual programs by pushing buttons on their converters, right up to the moment when the programming is shown, will greatly facilitate impulse buying of programs. This development, in turn, may be a major factor in fostering the spread of interactive converter technology throughout the industry.

Meter reading and energy management

Reading water and gas meters in subscriber homes is another function that can be performed using the subscriber cable network. Development of services in this area has been slow, however. Among other things, progress has been retarded by the fact that not all homes subscribe to cable. But equipment to perform such functions is being developed and demonstrations are underway.

Datavision Company of Roseville, Michigan, has developed an interface device (modem) that can retrofit water meters for as little as $18 and gas meters for $35. The company plans to use its equipment in Cox Cable's St. Clair Shores, Michigan, system and in Teleprompter's Grosse Pointe and Dearborn, Michigan, systems. Other companies actively involved in meter reading experiments include Adams-Russell (Boston suburbs), Continental Cable (Springfield and Brockton, Massachusetts), and Comcast (Clinton Township, Michigan).

Comcast began a 6-month experiment in October 1981 involving the installation of 50 units of a modem developed by E-Com in its Clinton, Michigan, system that will allow the city water department to generate monthly bills. The modem used in this demonstration sells for $200; the company expects to produce a second-generation device in 1982 that will sell for $75. Comcast has stated to the Clinton Water Utility that they expect a "worst case" cost of $3 per meter. In another test, 100 homes in Omnicom Cablevision's system in Northville, Michigan, are participating in a demonstration using Systems & Support, Inc.'s Datalert terminals to read consumer water meters and to communicate with a central computer via the interactive system. The project uses meters and automatic reading registers manufactured by Neptune Water Meter Company.

Energy management systems have been offered in institutional network bids in recent major franchise competitions. Studies conducted by energy consultants have indicated that municipalities and major commercial users can achieve substantial savings through use of such systems. Many analysts believe, however, that such systems are not likely to be economically viable for installation in private homes in the near future.

Home information services

One of the long-awaited promises of cable is delivery of information to the home. In the next five years, industry seers predict that the contents of newspapers, local libraries, national databases, college courses, and possibly even mail will enter American homes via a wire. This will be made possible by addressable converters with numeric keypads resembling pocket calculators and by the spread of home computers connected to the cable. Information stored in regional or national computers will be made accessible in the home through a combination of cable, telephone, and possibly satellite connections. These home information services are expected to be convenient, energy-efficient, and competitively priced with alternatives. These types of services are still being developed, however, and will not be generally available on cable until the mid- to late-1980s.

Various home information services are currently available or on trial in England, France, and Canada. Teletext, or one-way service, is usually encoded and transmitted "under" regular programming on standard broadcast channels. Such systems have been developed under the names of Ceefax and ORACLE in Britain, Antiope in France, and TV Ontario and Telidon in Canada. Other systems often called videotex provide the user with a direct link to a computer via telephone or cable lines. Prestel in Britain, Teletel in France, and VISTA in Canada are examples of this type of system.

Teletext and videotex

Teletext is a one-way form of communication. Several hundred individual frames of information are continuously transmitted, round-robin fashion, so that the entire sequence is repeated every few seconds. The frames of information are accommodated on a portion of the standard television signal called the vertical blanking interval, which is normally invisible. Every TV channel can carry a teletext round-robin in addition to a regular TV picture. The home viewer, using an interface device with a numeric keypad, searches through menus of subjects, narrowing down the search by accessing increasingly specific categories. These services also can be received by home computers linked to the cable.

Videotex is an interactive technology; there is no transmission until the subscriber requests it. Instead of intercepting frames of information being transmitted over TV channels in continuous cycles, the videotex user summons to the home screen frames of information that are stored in a computer. To do this, the user transmits the appropriate questions or numbers to the computer, stating what is wanted, and the computer responds by sending the information downstream to that terminal only. As with teletext, videotex can be implemented by home computers, which offer greater flexibility and ease of access to computerized data. A discussion of two main differences between teletext and videotex follows.

Capacity   The two systems vary greatly in capacity. Videotex has a capacity for far more information than teletext because it gives the user direct access to the central computer. Teletext offers a limited number of pages, which are cycled downstream in sequence; the viewer selects a page only from those sent. The response time required for the requested page to be delivered imposes a practical limit on teletext capacity of approximately 400 pages, whereas videotex has a theoretically unlimited capacity to deliver information. The Prestel system currently offers 200,000 pages.

Format   Teletext can be sent either on a full channel or in the vertical blanking interval. Videotex requires a full channel. Different methods of "composing" each page require varying amounts of data. In the future, cable operators may have to weigh more efficient use of channel space against a greater capability for data when choosing which type of service to offer.

The two technologies also require different equipment to transmit and receive information.

Uses of teletext and viewdata

Newspapers   A survey performed by the British Broadcasting Corporation (BBC) teletext system, Ceefax, found that its most popular services were news headlines, television program guides, and word games. The electronic newspaper is likely to become a major service in the United States as well. According to the American Newspaper Publishers Association, at least 70 newspapers were providing local cable systems with material as of February 1982, and such service is swiftly accelerating. Channels dedicated to newspaper-provided material are often leased by the newspaper. Content is provided by character generators that provide "news crawls" on full channels. Experiments with "electronic publishing" are underway in several areas across the country.

In Park Cities, Texas, Sammons Cable has begun marketing an electronic news service it began to develop in 1980. Warner-Amex's system in Columbus, Ohio, is the site of a news project involving 11 newspapers, and a new venture involves satellite-delivered news from a service called Home Link Communications.

National databases   News and information are being provided by emerging national public databases such as The Source, CompuServe, the New York Times, Dow Jones, and Reuters News Service. The Source is the heart of Cox's proposed INDAX text service, whereas CompuServe will provide the basis for Warner-Amex's next information retrieval tests. The range of information available in these public databases is already large and is continuing to grow. News summaries and analyses; financial information; national, State, and local political information; shopping services such as Comp-U-Star; stock analysis; business publications abstracts; electronic mail; private teleconferencing; access to encyclopedias; consumer information; movie, book, and record reviews; word games; and medical and health information are all available on public databases.

Local databases   Some cable operators plan to develop locally and community-oriented databases, with an opportunity for community input through either access or local origination channels. Some companies have offered to place keyboards for community use in libraries, schools, government buildings, and other public places for public input and updating.

Assuming that hardware is developed, programming and software will be crucial components of information services. Many databases exist apart from cable, but these, like the hardware, must be adapted for cable in order to be useful. They must be technically compatible and "user friendly."

Captioning   One text service of particular social benefit is captioning. The same technology that encodes data on the vertical blanking interval for teletext can provide captioning for the hearing impaired, who number 14 million to 16 million of the U.S. population. The National Captioning Institute (NCI) currently offers this service, marketing decoders through Sears for reception of "closed" captioning. Many local groups provide "open" captioning, which does not require a special decoder to be received.

NCI is believed to be working toward a licensing agreement with cable operators for its captioned programming, so that subscribers who wish to receive captioning will no longer have to purchase a $275 decoder unit. NCI provides approximately 40 hours of closed-captioned programs per week in conjunction with ABC, NBC, and PBS. The NCI hearing-impaired audience is estimated at 150,000.

CBS, NBC, and AT&T are testing alternative forms of text delivery, which will probably be adaptable for captioning. One barrier to swifter development of this service is the lack of standardization in the text field. Decoders will develop quickly at reasonable prices as soon as a standard prevails.

QUBE

The most established of enhanced services is Warner-Amex's QUBE service in Columbus, Ohio. This service began as an opinion polling and pay-per-view service in 1977 and has since expanded to include home security, home banking, and computerized access to newspapers and other information services. A home energy management system is currently under development.

The Columbus system has approximately 50,000 subscribers; of these, 34,000 take the QUBE option. QUBE is the top tier of the Columbus cable system; two other tiers are available at lower monthly rates. The basic monthly rate for the QUBE tier is $11.95, with additional charges for usage-sensitive pay and information services.

The QUBE service consists of ten regular broadcast channels, ten "community" channels on which opinion polling takes place, and ten pay-per-view premium channels that offer old and new films, cultural events, and college courses. The price for each pay-per-view program ranges between 50 cents and $3, and viewers are allowed a two-minute grace period of viewing before the "meter" starts running. A parental lockout device is available for these premium channels.

The QUBE converter consists of buttons for each of the 30 channels plus the five response buttons. These buttons are used to answer yes/no and multiple choice questions on local talk, variety, and public affairs shows. For instance, "Columbus Alive," a local talk show, measures viewer opinions on well-known guests. A consumer information program enables subscribers to register satisfaction or dissatisfaction with various products. Opinions also can be measured on political issues, as when 7,000 viewers responded to questions after a speech by

President Carter. The following services also are available with extra equipment:

1. A home security service consisting of burglar and fire alarm sensors and a medical alert button. Installation costs between $99 and $400, with a monthly charge of approximately $10.
2. A computer service offering 10 local and national newspapers, stock and financial information, video games, and electronic mail delivery. This service requires a home computer. CompuServe connect time is about 9 cents per minute.

INDAX

A more recent development in enhanced services is Cox Cable's INDAX system, which will enable subscribers to shop, bank, and receive news and information via cable. The service is being tested in San Diego and will be built in Omaha, New Orleans, Tucson, and Vancouver, Washington. In Omaha, INDAX users will pay $10.50 for basic service plus $5.95 for INDAX.

Rather than developing the entire array of interactive services itself, Cox contracts with specialized service providers. Source Telecomputing Corp. of McLean, Virginia, provides a 700-"page" teletext service offering news, travel schedules, and other information. (Future systems will carry The Source's expanded two-way service, which includes electronic message delivery.) Unlike two-way text services, the teletext service is billed on a flat fee rather than a per-use basis.

Two other components of the system, shopping and banking, are provided by Viewmart and HomServ, respectively. These organizations make all arrangements between the subscribers and the bankers and merchants. For instance, Viewmart provides a text "menu" of merchandise organized in six categories: "Special of the Week," "Brand Names," "Stores," "Products," "Services," and "Gift Ideas." The viewer then selects the desired item from the menu and enters a credit card or authorizing number on the INDAX keypad. HomServ functions as a similar liaison with area banks.

The interactive converters used by Cox also make possible instant access to pay-per-view movies, eliminating the need to write or phone in orders ahead of time. Subscribers can also program their converters to block out movies automatically based on their MPAA ratings.

The two-way capabilities of the INDAX system expand subscribers' options from simple responses to detailed requests. Whereas QUBE subscribers could only answer "yes" or "no" to a specific item being advertised, the INDAX system gives subscribers greater selection and versatility.

Privacy and other issues

The proliferation of two-way interactive cable systems and services such as shopping and banking at home have raised many concerns regarding subscriber privacy. Additional problems are raised by the polling capabilities of interactive systems. From a technological point of view, nothing prevents the computers at the system's headend from compiling the results of such polls on an individual basis and thereby generating profiles of the points of view and attitudes of each subscriber.

The security of financial transactions, the protection of subscribers against commercial exploitation through monitoring of their viewing habits, and the possible interest of law enforcement authorities in the behavior of various citizens raise important questions that have not yet been fully addressed in a national dialog. Thus, many recently franchised cities have required cable operators to protect subscriber privacy by prohibiting the operator from unauthorized use of subscriber data.

In addition to privacy, several legal, technical, and economic questions will have to be answered as enhanced and interactive services become widespread. Much of the hardware associated with the delivery of interactive services is still being developed. In some instances, the hardware problem is generic to the technology; the lack of industrywide standards for teletext and videotex is an example of this problem.

Software development for many services is also in preliminary stages. Consumer acceptance will evolve only when adequate software to fulfill consumer needs has been developed.

Many economic questions must be asked about the viability of enhanced and interactive services in the marketplace. The hardware and software for many of these services is costly, and consumer demand is as yet undetermined. Many services may not find wide acceptance. The more complex the service is, the greater the price tag will be, causing all subscribers to pay for capability that may be commercially attractive to only a few.

It is difficult to predict where cable will fit in the information delivery business. Many potentially competitive technologies have not developed far enough to provide analysts with a clear idea of how information will travel in the future and what it will cost.

Security and Fire Alarm Services

John Mansell

In recent years, cable companies have begun to offer burglar and fire alarm services to subscriber homes via cable, a response to the increasing demand for security and fire alarm systems in general. Experience to date indicates that security service may be a profitable field for cable companies; if so, it will provide a source of revenue for costly two-way systems in major markets and possibly an impetus for the further development and use of two-way cable hardware.

At present, only a small percentage of U.S. homes have centrally monitored security alarm systems. Many factors, including rising crime rates, psychological factors, geography, and economics are stimulating a more widespread demand for security services.

Central station monitoring can also improve firefighting services. Thousands perish each year because firefighters are not called quickly enough to contain a blaze. According to the U.S. Fire Administration, indirect monetary losses from fires are more than $200 million a year.

System considerations

The strength of a cable system for monitoring fire and burglar alarm systems is its ability to disseminate information from a single source to a large number of remote points. The technology of the subscriber network, however, raises problems that must be solved for successful security operations.

Reprinted with permission from *The Community Medium*, volume 1 of *CTIC Cablebooks*, edited by Nancy Jesuale with Ralph Lee Smith (Arlington, Va.: Cable Television Information Center, 1982).

In a cable system, downstream video signals are usually transmitted at frequencies ranging from 50 to 440 MHz. Alarm signals and other data transmissions, which use a much more limited amount of bandwidth, typically travel upstream at frequencies of from 5 to 30 MHz. These return signals often face a more hostile electronic environment because of shortwave, CB, and AM radio transmission on frequencies in the same range. If any of these outside signals penetrate the layers of protective shielding and insulation of the cable, the "noise ingress" can contaminate the quality of the return signal. This interference does not significantly disturb the quality of video pictures, but it can threaten the integrity of alarm signals and other data transmissions. Some two-way cable systems, such as Warner-Amex in Columbus, Ohio, and Rogers Cablesystems in Syracuse, N.Y., use a technology called bridger switching to prevent the cumulative buildup of noise. In effect, the cable system is sectionized; part of the city is polled while another part of switched off.

Security service has also placed pressure on cable operators to increase reliability and maintenance of their systems in other respects. Power outages caused by lightning, ice storms, and other natural causes might be tolerable for entertainment services, but are unacceptable in alarm monitoring. Consequently, many cable operators believe standby power and a backup redundant mode of transmission are critical. Warner-Amex, for example, has a digital communicator built into all its control panels. If the cable signal cannot get through, the digital signal is automatically sent over a regular telephone line to the cable central station.

Use of digital communicators also enables cable companies to market security devices outside their franchise territories. Indeed, several cable companies have 50 percent or more of their security customers linked by digital dialers in areas not yet wired for cable or beyond the franchise boundaries.

Status monitoring and standby power As a signal travels along cable, its strength fades until it is boosted by amplifiers scattered throughout the system. Because technical performance of the cable system tends to degrade as the equipment ages, some sort of remote status-monitoring system is important to track the performance of the amplifiers. It is also important to have an uninterruptible power supply in order to minimize disruptions during power dips and surges. But, even the best status-monitoring and maintenance system cannot prevent weather from sometimes affecting the supply of power to the system. Therefore, battery backup standby power should be provided for amplifiers where power is inserted into the system.

Cable security operating experience   Security systems have been sold to cable operators in at least 63 major systems that eventually will be able to serve 3.7 million homes. In addition, cable security systems in 26 planned developments will someday pass 200,000 new homes. The average cable security customer pays $906 for installation and $16 a month for monitoring. Cable TV security subscribership in the first half of 1981 grew at a rate of about 650 homes per month, from 12,334 to 17,290 connections, an increase of 3,955 (32 percent) since January 1, 1981. As of January 1982, systems were operating in 17 cities and eight planned developments.

Cable security equipment   Only a handful of companies currently manufacture cable security equipment, but there soon will be nearly a dozen suppliers, including Jerrold, Pioneer Communications, and Scientific-Atlanta. The leading supplier is Tocom, which produces three systems that have capacities of 1,000, 3,000, and 128,000 subscribers. Most cable companies purchase a $57,000 computer that has an initial capacity of 3,000 subscribers and is expandable in 8,000-subscriber increments (at a cost of $40,000 per increment) up to 128,000 subscribers.

Tocom's central station computer polls each home every six seconds. In effect, the computer asks if everything is in order. Intrusion, smoke, and heat sensors are installed in the subscriber's home, along with a control panel and a home terminal. Sensors are wired into the control panel. In an emergency, an alarm is transmitted to the central station where name, address, telephone number, type of alarm, and medical history are computerized and instantly printed out.

The equipment of other manufacturers works a little differently. The CableBus system uses less bandwidth and polls more slowly, which makes it more compatible with existing alarm industry equipment. Another manufacturer, Control-Com, has equipment that works even with one-way cable systems. It uses regionalized pole-mounted microprocessors to collect and poll information from the home. Those microprocessors, in turn, are polled by a master computer that relays alarm information to the headend. This technique solves the noise ingress problem. Detroit-based Datavision concentrates on providing security to condominiums and apartment complexes. General Instruments' Jerrold division is developing a "frequency agile" system that will use several different return frequencies to eliminate noise ingress problems.

The Syracuse test

Rogers Cablesystems conducted a free, 1,000-home test of cable TV security in Syracuse, N.Y., from October 1980 to October 1981. Randomly selected and volunteer homes throughout the city were given smoke alarms and emergency panic buttons. During the course of the experiment, 472 police calls and 769 fire alarms emanated from the test homes as follows.

Police	Fire
73 valid emergencies	15 lives saved/property
288 minor incidents	damage averted
90 tests or child play	740 minor, environmental,
10 system fault	or friendly fires
11 appliance related	14 system malfunctions

The cable security alarm signals in Syracuse are transmitted directly to the city's public safety building, where the resident's name and address are printed on display terminals. Then a computer automatically places the dispatcher at the public safety building in telephone contact with the residence. This procedure takes very little time and cuts the cost of false alarms.

Syracuse fire chief, Tom Hanlon, says the system has proven itself and calls the experiment a success. City officials and consultants plan to evaluate the service to determine if it should be made available citywide. The evaluation will focus on system performance, public attitudes, price, elasticity of demand, and cost-effectiveness.

Public policy concerns

False alarms   Improving public safety by encouraging the use of security alarm systems must be balanced against the potential cost and wastefulness resulting from possible increases in false alarms. As the percentage of homes with alarm systems increases, inevitably false alarms will increase as well.

Most cable TV systems that offer burglar and fire alarm services mitigate the false alarm problem by using a telephone call-back procedure. When an alarm signal is received at the central station, the monitoring operator immediately telephones the home. If there is no answer or if the person answering the phone gives the wrong identification code, the proper authorities are immediately notified and dispatched.

A January 1980 U.S. Fire Administration study entitled "Remote Detections and Alarms for Residences: the Woodlands System," by David Moore, concluded that there "appears to be a trend of fewer fire losses" in Woodlands, Texas, homes that have the Tocom system. The study noted, however, that statistically significant conclusions could not be made about the system's effectiveness because the number of fires in the sample was too small.

Competition and access   The existing alarm industry views cable TV as both an opportunity and a threat. The public's positive perception of cable and the cable industry's proven marketing prowess could help the alarm industry, which has long been plagued by a poor public image. Unlike many of the small alarm dealers in a community, cable operators have credibility and a firm financial foundation. Their multimillion dollar investment guarantees a long-term relationship with the community. They see an opportunity to bring to the security industry the maturity it has not yet attained on its own.

Because most cable companies lack the technical and operating experience of alarm companies, and the alarm dealers lack the marketing capabilities and capital of cable, joint ventures would appear to be an attractive option to both industries. In many cities, however, the alarm industry is guarding its position in an effort to preempt cable from being anything more than a carrier of alarm signal transmissions.

Alarm associations in Indianapolis, Indiana, Jefferson County, Kentucky, and Nashville, Tennessee, have successfully lobbied to prevent cable companies from providing security alarm services. In other communities, such as Omaha, Nebraska, and St. Louis County, Missouri, alarm dealers have threatened lawsuits against both cable companies and municipal franchising authorities. They claim that the cable franchise is a *de facto* monopoly giving the cable operator an inherent competitive advantage—the ability to advertise at lower rates and to use entertainment-related revenues to subsidize security services.

Omaha alarm companies have gone so far as to claim the city acted beyond its authority in granting the cable company the use of city rights-of-way for the provision of alarm services. Alarm dealers emphasize that cable franchises often bar cable companies from the sale and repair of TV receivers, leaving that business to established TV repair companies who already provide the service. They argue that cable should serve as a transmission facility and leave installation, monitoring, and service to the private security business. In effect, alarm companies want access to the cable system on the same terms as all potential users.

The issues raised by the alarm dealers pose a number of technical, economic, and public policy questions that are difficult to resolve. First, the current state of the art may allow only for a limited number of alarm companies to tie their central stations into the cable system. Second, a cable company risks liability and damage to its reputation by doing business with a poorly managed or undercapitalized third party. Third, the degree to which municipalities may impose common carrier[1] status upon cable (if at all) is unclear in light of conflicting court decisions.

Recently, New Jersey Bell Telephone petitioned the New Jersey Office of Cable TV to assert common carrier jurisdiction over cable security service when Cablevision of Bayonne requested certification to begin construction. New Jersey Bell asked the cable office to exercise to "the full extent" its authority, "including the incorporation of the public utility rate, cost and service principles, if appropriate, to insure maximum regulatory parity in the treatment of regulated suppliers of two-way communications services." Cable companies and their associations argued in reply that security is a nonessential service and that cable has no monopoly power either to discriminate among potential recipients or price its services excessively because such services are already available in the marketplace.

In the years to come, conflicts in the cable security field may produce rulings and precedents that will refine the legal status of leased access to cable and of the cable operator's exclusive right to offer services that others may also wish to offer over the facility.

1. Common carriers are service providers who are required by State and Federal regulators to allow access to their facilities on a first-come, first-served basis and who may not discriminate in pricing. Moreover, common carriers are prohibited from using their own facilities to deliver their own services on a preferred basis.

A New Institution

Victoria Gits

More accurately described as freebies, good-will gestures and franchise ploys in the past, institutional networks, say some industry observers, are destined to be to the cable industry in the '80s and the '90s what pay TV was in the '70s.

No major bid today is without its B Loop, CommNet, BEST-NET or ICN, in some cases backed by volumes of survey research attesting to the notion there is almost nothing AT&T can do that cable can't do cheaper, faster and better.

"The whole idea is futuristic," says Ann Kirschner, executive director of proposal development for Teleprompter, "But cable is so clearly an appropriate medium. This is the point where cable grows up and becomes a true communications medium."

Partially in response to the concerns of cities and their consultants, partially in recognition of the growing market for business communications, cable companies are working harder to prove the systems are not to be a drain on profits, but self-supporting, viable enterprises.

A look at some more recent institutional network proposals illustrates the variety of approach:

Warner Cable Corp., Pittsburgh, Pa., Oct. 1979 In the first wave of major market bids to include an I-net, Warner went out on a limb to offer a dual subscriber cable (825 miles), plus a separate, combined institutional/business cable (120 to 150 miles).

Storer Cable Communications, Scottsdale, Ariz., May 1981 In

© 1982, Titsch Communications, Inc. All rights reserved. Reprinted from the April 5 issue of **CableVision**, with permission.

addition to a dual cable 400 MHz subscriber net, Storer bid a 400 MHz, mid-split, 95-mile cable carrying both commercial and public institutional signals. A fourth, shorter cable would be reserved for government use in the Scottsdale Mall area.

Teleprompter, Brooklyn, N.Y., Dec. 1980   Teleprompter's bid, ultimately withdrawn, proposed five discrete cables, one for a dual cable subscriber network (1,400 miles); one 54-channel capacity cable for an institutional network (490 miles) paralleled by an equally long, separate business communications cable; plus a special Borough Loop (4.5 miles) serving the downtown business core.

United Cable Television, Denver, Colo., Sept. 1981   United bid a dual-cable subscriber network of 1,300 miles, a separate third cable, 383 miles long, reserved for nonprofit organizations and businesses, plus a 116-mile, business-only, downtown loop.

Maclean Hunter and Times Mirror, Montgomery County, Md., Jan. 1982   In this market there are more than 200 employers with at least 100 employees each; 40 percent of the major firms are high-technology companies. The request for proposals was unusual in that it demanded not only an institutional network, but also one that could support itself. The result was Maclean Hunter's two-cable I-net: one 70-mile cable dedicated to the private sector only and a second, 350-mile cable shared by both public and commercial concerns. Times Mirror followed through with mass coverage: over 5,000 miles of cable structured in separate dual-cable residential (1,697 miles) and dual-cable institutional (1,728 miles) networks. A separate high traffic cable was offered to serve businesses along the I-270/Bethesda-Silver Spring corridor. TM put the initial capital and operating cost at $15 million.

The investment assessed

The strength of some of the institutional networks being proposed today attests to the cable industry's awareness there is more to communications than delivering more sports, more movies and more fluff.

"Nobody has proven definitively that the need justifies the capital expense which is manifested in these offers," says Berge Ayvazian, Kalba Bowen Associates, Cambridge, Mass., author of the Times Mirror proposal for an institutional package in Montgomery County. Nevertheless, Ayvazian is confident the investment is sound.

Set up as a separate entity with its own balance sheet and

staff, the Times Mirror I-net is projected to net $2.2 million in year six on gross revenues of $7.7 million. The equity commitment is in excess of $5 million; debt is $13 million and is to be substantially repaid by year 10.

It wasn't always viewed as a business, Ayvazian said, but rather as a competitive edge in franchising. "We weren't thinking of revenues or financial self-sufficiency (prior to Montgomery County)." Nor was practically anyone else in the business.

A comparison of Indianapolis bids revealed similar weaknesses. Ayvazian said: "Lots of bells and whistles with very little understanding of what the needs or the revenues might be." To Ayvazian and his peer consultants it began to seem a little ridiculous that investing $2 million to $10 million should be looked upon simply as the cost of winning a franchise.

By the time Montgomery County presented itself to cable entrepreneurs the climate had changed. Consultants, as well as decision-makers, began to be concerned that the institutional networks—which had by now graduated from simple, abbreviated loops to full-blown systems-within-the-system—would do serious damage to the bottom line.

Thus, the challenge was to translate the mere hunch there was a lucrative market in commercial applications into a quantitative, dollars-and-cents statement.

Kalba Bowen identified five major service areas of interest to Montgomery County users: low-speed data transmission; high-speed data transmission; video transmission for program distribution and teleconferencing; electronic message services; and security services. By far the greatest revenue source (60 percent of the total) was high- and low-speed data transmission.

Cable consultant Carl Pilnick, president of Telecommunications Management Corp., has long been convinced of the viability of combined institutional and business networks, separate from subscriber nets. In fact, he said, he was probably one of the first to recommend that cities ask for them. Among the earliest to make the I-net part of an RFP were Portland, Ore., and Dayton, Ohio, in 1973, Pilnick said.

Pilnick is highly skeptical, however, that cable companies are committed to making I-nets work. "It's evolved more as a franchising ploy than anything else," Pilnick said.

"They are very nervous about competing with the phone company. They think at some point later, the phone company will come in and undercut them. In addition, they are worried (if they get into the business) they will be labeled as a common carrier," Pilnick said.

Furthermore, they are somewhat lacking in the proper attitude: "They are more interested in selling HBO and making a lot of money without doing very much work." Pay TV is easy to sell, contends Pilnick, "but banks and corporations have very sophisticated data needs requiring a higher grade of engineering and marketing effort."

Pilnick is convinced that now is the time to make the commitment. "My question is what's going to happen when somebody does Premiere all over again? (A reference to the likelihood one pay network will lock up exclusive movie titles, as Getty Oil, MCA, Fox, Columbia and Paramount tried to do in 1980 for their court-aborted network.) What if pay TV becomes less profitable?" The cable industry should be looking for other sources and the commercial sector is ripe. "In many cases, you don't even have to convince them," Pilnick says, "cable offers a cheaper way to do what they already are doing."

It is worth noting that Pilnick takes a dim view of combining both institutional and subscriber services on the same cable. "It's a gimmick. They say it's better, but that's nonsense. They just don't want to build a separate system. When they make it fail, they'll convert it to entertainment services." Among the advantages of a separate cable, Pilnick cites reverse capability and security.

Institutional networks are still so new there are virtually none around to evaluate. Innumerable operators, of course, have successfully used cable in educational settings, which is one form of institutional use. Experience is sparse in the use of cable in the broader sense of data, voice and text transmission.

One enterprise that comes closest to serving as evidence in favor of cable in the business users' market is Manhattan Cable Television (MCTV), a subsidiary of American Television and Communications (ATC). Since 1974, MCTV has been in the business of providing high-speed data transmissions on a nine-mile-long cable in the heart of New York City's financial community.

According to Carl Gamballo, director of corporate development, the marketing campaign is picking up steam. "Right now awareness is low," he said, "but we are beginning to make a more concentrated effort." He estimated 1981 revenues in the neighborhood of $1 million.

One can also look to Satellite Business Systems (SBS), which has completed a test of its coast-to-coast communications network utilizing local cable systems, microwave links and satellite. A venture costing some $600 million so far, SBS was founded on the promise of high-speed data communications networks. To date the results have not been entirely encouraging. In 1981, revenues were not quite up to $5 million—a long reach away from the goal of $250 million in 1982.

ATC and WACCI moves

Now that institutional networks are a *fait accompli* in many
markets—whether they were conceived out of a desire to be one-
up on the competition or in anticipation of developing new
markets—operators are engaged in making a go of them.

ATC, for example, gets credit for implementing the first
institutional network in Reading, Pa. As Reading's veteran cable
guru Earl Haydt puts it, institutional networking isn't new, it's
just a new word for what Berks Cable has been doing all along,
and doing quite well, despite the limitations of a 12-channel
system.

ATC took the Reading concept one step further in its 1978
proposal for Kansas City, Mo., where the company bid its first
separate institutional loop. Sixty miles long, with eleven upstream and 21 downstream channels, the network connects 52
institutions, including hospitals, libraries, colleges and police. It
is nearly complete now, and set for turn-on in summer 1982. No
business link is under consideration at this time.

Cyd Slayton, Kansas City's director of community pro-
gramming/institutional network, has found getting the project
off the ground is a slow process, requiring resolution of diverse
vested interests. It has taken a year just to lay the groundwork.
Hospitals are likely to be the first on board, because they have
staffed, in-house studios, video experience and are aware of the
benefits of cablecasting for professional education and live
teleconferencing.

Back at home in Denver, where ATC in partnership with
Daniels and Associates pledged a showcase system, the company
is promoting the latest style in institutional networking: the self-
supporting system. It has a snappy name, BEST-NET, for
Business Educational, Shopping and Transaction Network and
is designed to serve both profit and nonprofit institutions con-
currently. The loop is to be 400 miles long, with 38-channel
capacity downstream and 17 upstream. It will follow the path of
the subscriber trunk and connect the downtown business core to
outlying business parks.

(On Feb. 22, 1982, Mile Hi Cablevision, a joint venture of
ATC, Daniels & Associates and 22 local investors, was designated best bidder in the Denver franchise competition.)

Proposed BEST-NET services, in addition to the basic data
transmission, video conferencing, surveillance and electronic
mail, include 13 novel informational tiers geared to local needs:
SkiColorado; PostalDenver; AgriDenver; MedDenver; Petro-
Denver, etc.

Based on capital expense estimated at $10,000 per street
mile ($4 million), the breakeven point is projected in the sixth

year. Financial *pro forma* show institutional revenues at $7 million in year six and $10 million in year 10.

Trygve Myhren, chairman and CEO at ATC, said institutional networks are an "important ingredient," in situations where the downtown is being built, but he was reluctant to offer a ringing endorsement of the profit potential. "There aren't many in operation now to look at," Myhren said. "You can't make a spirited prediction." In the near term, "It is not as big an effort as advertising, pay-per-view, security and local newspaper arrangements," he said.

While the Denver BEST-NET is still a long way from becoming a reality, Warner Cable Corp. of Pittsburgh is but a year away from completing a 120- to 150-mile-long I-net linking schools, municipal buildings, police and fire departments, as well as businesses.

Warner is taking an aggressive approach in regard to cornering the business community and is now in the process of negotiating contracts with several corporations.

Elizabeth Olenbush, manager of institutional network operations for Warner in Pittsburgh, spends most of her time educating people about the more exotic uses of cable. "Pittsburgh is surrounded by 12-channel systems," she said. "They don't understand I am interested in something besides television. . . . The biggest problem is getting people to understand that one of the enormous benefits is they can integrate voice, data and video and that it might be an advantage over having to go to three and four separate suppliers."

Olenbush's experience points up the difficulties cable companies are likely to have in marketing new services to corporations that already are large users of sophisticated communications techniques: "Their internal communications functions are not consolidated. There has never been a cost-effective method of doing all these things at once. Institutions have developed systems that make video, data and voice separate functions handled by different departments. They haven't had to deal with each other," Olenbush said.

Nevertheless, Pittsburgh is the third largest corporate headquarters center in the nation and should prove an attractive market.

Some indication of Warner's commitment to the potential of institutional and business networking was the appointment of Tom Rush as vice president, commercial services in Oct. 1981. He was formerly market development director for SBS for seven years.

Rush sees a growing demand for high-speed video conferencing in the future—a demand sparked by current pressure for increased productivity in the workplace. Among the first business customers signing up for cable, he said, are most likely to be large corporations, in particular banks, with facilities in several locations in a city. Two or three years down the road, he predicts image-oriented data using high-definition television will come into prominence, along with cross-town private telephone packages. In the medical area, hospitals will use cable to access large computers in distant locations.

Make or break

Whether the currently modish characterization of institutional networks as separate, self-supporting entities is merely a dream, a case of technology getting ahead of itself, or an instance of franchise nonsense is the larger question to be answered in the '80s.

In the meantime, the greatest competitive threat is an aggressive push by local telephone companies. Another thorny matter is the prospect of common carrier designation. An ATC examination of case law on the subject points to a decision in which the court held cable systems to be common carriers, if engaged in offering two-way, point-to-point, non-video, data communications services. Another ruling held that a non-cable firm that sought to transmit digitized data to designated recipients was said to be a common carrier under terms of the 1934 Communications Act. The FCC also has established that where telephone companies own cable systems, the cable systems would be treated as common carriers.

Howard Gan, general counsel for Cable Television Information Center, said the cable operator probably could avoid the designation by showing willingness to enter into agreements with a variety of service providers. If they engage in shortsighted thinking and exclusive deals, Gan said, there will be pressure from other very powerful service industries.

It is not an easy task to push beyond the bounds of the reliable and lucrative niche cable has carved as entertainment provider. What's more, it could be a critical drain on cash in an era when construction budgets will be pushing the maximum. How the industry responds to the test could be a make or break proposition. It could be the dawning of the day cable grows up.

Institutional
Networks

Thomas E. Wolfsohn

An institutional network is a cable network, separate from cable subscriber services, that provides nonentertainment transmission services for businesses, public agencies, and community institutions. Most often, an institutional network uses a separate cable, which passes through a limited area of the municipality; including commercial clusters and municipal, education, and health facilities. An institutional network's path may parallel the subscriber network partially or completely, or the subscriber cable may include dedicated bandwidth to supply institutional transmission services.

The concept of a special institutional cable system grew out of the cable television industry's recent expansion into major urban areas. Cable operators, searching for new services and sources of revenue, were able to take advantage of technological innovations that allowed cable systems to build high-capacity, two-way systems with computer switching capabilities. Thus, cable systems could potentially serve as information pipelines in an urban area, transporting data, video, and voice to discrete locations passed by the cable. To conserve capacity on the subscriber cable and to limit the number of additional expensive plant miles built to carry institutional services, cable operators began to look at building a separate cable simultaneously with the subscriber cable.

Institutional network design allows switching at the head-end so that transmissions originating on the institutional net-

Reprinted with permission from *The Community Medium*, volume 1 of *CTIC Cablebooks*, edited by Nancy Jesuale with Ralph Lee Smith (Arlington, Va.: Cable Television Information Center, 1982).

work can be delivered to the subscriber network when desired. Transmissions can be "scrambled" as well, so that only designated locations will receive the information. Thus, transactions, records, videotapes, and "phone" conversations can be delivered only to the institutional user for whom they are intended.

The birth of these new institutional networks coincides with the rise of distributed computer networks which are supplanting time-sharing systems keyed to large mainframe computers. The use of microprocessors throughout a system provides both increased memory and a higher total transaction rate. Institutional networks have emerged as a possible delivery mechanism for these new distributed computer networks.

As of early 1982, a large number of institutional network commitments had been made by cable companies, and development is underway. The few existing institutional networks are not fully utilized, however, and in most cases there have been no firm estimates of the nature and quantity of traffic to be generated.

Noncommercial institutional network services

It is too early to tell if institutional networks will be built with the level of capacity predicted. Cable's advantage over other transmission technologies is its multiplicity of channels and its capacity to carry broad-band video signals. It can also carry high-speed data at significantly reduced error rates. A brief description of proposed applications for institutional networks follows.

In-service training   Using a combination of video materials and cable's interactive potential, the need for employees to travel to training sessions may be significantly reduced. Prepackaged video training materials used in conjunction with simultaneous data, audio, or video hookups can allow standardized training to be delivered while workers remain on the job. For instance, a National Science Foundation/Michigan State University report states that in firefighting, daily training is the norm. Training officers' efforts are often interrupted, however, by fires and emergency calls. Also, special firefighters' schedules complicate training and recordkeeping activities. The report concluded that two-way cable is effective for higher firefighter instruction and that the cost of using two-way cable, under most circumstances, is lower than self-study or lecture methods.

Law enforcement   Institutional networks can serve as the transmission medium for numerous police functions. In New York City, a facsimile system transmits fingerprints, mugshots, and bail bonds. In Philadelphia, 26 precincts and district headquarters are linked to a studio in the police administration building. Three times a day, at shift changes, training, policy changes, directives, and "wanted" bulletins are communicated. Training tapes and films are transmitted at other times of the day. Closed-circuit arraignments are carried out from certain outlying district stations, making it easier to comply with a State law that requires arraignments to occur within six hours of incarceration. Although these examples do not use cable institutional networks, this type of communication is well suited to institutional network application.

Law enforcement officers can also communicate with specifically targeted populations over the institutional network, allowing public education and community relations efforts via cable. For instance, officers can "visit" classrooms, senior citizens, and retailers, providing information on burglary and assault prevention, alcohol abuse, narcotics, and shoplifting.

Remote video surveillance and security systems Remote video surveillance is a security function well suited to cable. Cameras can be placed in strategic locations, with the video signal transmitted to a control center over the cable. Remote-sensing devices designed for intrusion monitoring and fire detection can be installed in institutions and businesses on the cable, and their signals can be monitored by a control center. These types of services are being made available on subscriber networks as well. (Security systems are discussed in another article.)

Status and control services Telemetry, or electronic monitoring, is now being used in a few cable systems to test its efficacy in water level and usage monitoring, residential utility meter monitoring, energy load management, and sewer pumping and treatment facilities control. Plymouth Township, Pennsylvania, uses Tilbury Cable Company's cable network for an Interactive Systems 3M-designed, automated microprocessor-controlled sewer pumping station monitoring system. The use of cable insures constant monitoring and virtually eliminates false alarms common to systems that use leased telephone lines. Likewise, the city of Valparaiso, Florida, controls 17 pumping stations in its water system via the cable network.

Industrial parks, factories, and high-technology industries passed by an institutional loop could all benefit from substantial energy savings with a cable-run energy management system. Municipally run utilities could experience substantial savings by offering peakload management over the cable system.

Most energy management and telemetry experiments are currently being conducted on the subscriber network, however. The convenience of the subscriber network for such types of services argues for the insertion of the institutional network services on the subscriber cable or for a fully parallel institutional network; however, this configuration is cost-prohibitive in many communities.

Delivery of services to isolated populations   In every urban area, groups of individuals live in relative isolation, with limited transportation and limited incomes. These include senior citizens in senior homes, juveniles in institutions, handicapped citizens in institutions, and citizens who are hospitalized or have limited physical mobility. Many special institutional network services can be offered to these populations. Agencies that provide municipal services to these groups can be linked directly to the institutions, making it possible for caseworkers to make more frequent "visits."

In many cases, services can be delivered electronically. Medicare and food stamp certification, Social Security information, housing information, bus schedules, and notices of special hearings or events are examples of the types of services which could be delivered at low cost over the institutional network. However, before "teleservices" become commonplace, techniques to safeguard client privacy will have to be implemented.

Isolated populations can originate messages and programming over the network to other institutions and to subscribers. A case in point exists in Reading, Pennsylvania, where for several years senior citizens have created live two-way video programming between senior centers, high schools, city departments, and home viewers to discuss issues, have sing-alongs, or simply talk with each other. This programming is "open" to subscribers because their cable system does not use scrambling techniques.

Social services administration   In addition to the active service delivery described above, social services can use the institutional network to relieve the paper transfer of such data as client eligibility, payment, tracking, and attendance records. Using electronic data processing for such tasks can allow rapid retrieval at any site connected to a departmental database. With the addition of facsimile capability, signatures, forms, and other documents that need to be verified also can be handled via the institutional network.

Database delivery   Automated systems for circulation and cataloging of information can easily interface with a cable TV network. Public libraries have access to databases and specialized information sources that can be even more valuable when linked to other institutions that either use or provide data. Because libraries have traditionally been in the information business, they are often the lead agency in coordinating the municipality's marriage with cable technology.

As institutional networks develop, it is likely that geographically dispersed public agencies will interconnect both to meet their own operational needs and to transfer information to other units of government. New databases will be created to centralize information on such subjects as assessments, housing, public assistance, and census data. Access for institutional terminal points to dedicated municipal channels will allow swift information access at lower transmission costs than traditional leased phone lines.

Major users of the institutional network are expected to include educators and health institutions, government agencies, and local commercial institutions that depend on computerized information and swift and accurate transfers and responses.

Commercial services

Data applications In the beginning stages of any institutional network, most commercial applications are likely to be data transmission services. The transactional businesses—finance institutions, retailers, and the travel industry in particular—depend on the transfer of specialized information to geographically dispersed branches or retailers; such functions are well suited to cable institutional networks. The cable industry may also be able to reach the largely untapped market of small, local businesses with growing data processing needs that thus far have been "priced out" of data processing services.

Facsimile transmission services, as well as electronic mail and file retrieval systems will be directed at organizations which retain large volumes of records or require extensive paperwork. There are a number of "store and forward" methods in which documents can be handled electronically. At this point in the development of interface technology, however, most facsimile machines are configured to operate on dial-up telephone lines.

Video applications Video applications generally will require the greatest demands on bandwidth and dollar and human resources. Video teleconferencing permits remotely located groups or individuals to communicate, with savings in time and transportation. In addition to an interface device and a special room set aside for teleconferencing, standard control units provide for voice-activated video screen displays on receive and camera-activated transmit, with a rear- or front-projection screen. The full video aspect of teleconferencing permits transmission and exchange of graphics, in addition to permitting full visual contact between teleconferencing parties. Slow scan teleconferencing permits high resolution images to be transmitted, but it is not possible to follow rapid movement.

Most video teleconferencing is presently carried out in two modes. The first is transmission to hotel meeting rooms and conference centers by occasional users, such as sales organizations, for new product introductions or sales meetings and by associations, to reach their membership, and for training. The second is regularly scheduled teleconferencing by individual private corporations, many of which have their own facilities. Teleconferences in the first category are usually beamed by satellite; those in the second may use terrestrial telephone lines or satellite.

The basic signal path for satellite video teleconferences is (1) point of origination to (2) satellite station to (3) satellite transponder to (4) satellite stations to (5) viewing sites.

At origination sites, an institutional network might well provide an alternative to the microwave or telephone route to the uplink. At the receiving sites, in addition to providing a similar alternative route, the institutional network can connect additional local receive sites to extend participation in the teleconference.

Marketing and staff Communications managers are the first line customers for institutional network services, and to date they have demonstrated a "show me" attitude toward cable television. These professionals are looking for around-the-clock transmission capability, dependability (their operations will be seriously impaired if a system is "down" for long), and service standards equivalent to, or better than, those of the telephone companies.

Arguments for carrying out a needs ascertainment apply equally to public agencies and potential commercial customers. Market research aimed at identifying potential users can aid network management to set priorities for service applications and to design those services to accommodate existing equipment and operations. Beyond the ascertainment, institutional network management must maintain an ongoing public relations/ marketing campaign to educate and inform potential customers.

Cable television has developed quite differently from those communications technologies with which it is converging. Service has focused on signal amplifiers and passive devices (and only recently, more sophisticated converters), and marketing has been aimed at selling reception service and entertainment programming door-to-door to the residential customer. Institutional network management faces weightier service and marketing concerns. Highly qualified personnel will be required to work closely with customers as well as original equipment manufacturer staff on interface and terminal equipment problems.

Ratesetting

Most franchise proposals will offer to provide transmission and certain terminal equipment on the institutional network to public buildings at no charge. Many cable companies, however, are struggling with ratesetting policies for commercial use of the network. To date, rates for nonentertainment services offered on cable television are often set arbitrarily. Until several institutional networks are operational, rate patterns will probably not emerge.

There are several approaches to setting rates. One is to charge a flat rate, especially for video transmission, on a monthly or yearly basis. For shared-channel situations, either video or data, a flat rate might be less appropriate because it would not reflect levels of use. A schedule based on volume transmitted, that is, units of data or hours of video, would probably be more equitable. Just as utilities set "peak load" rates, institutional network pricing might be keyed to business hours or "prime" user time.

In addition to rates for time or bandwidth, institutional network management must also set rates for leasing interface and terminal equipment and offering technical assistance to customers.

A ratesetting philosophy must support any institutional network tariffs. In the case of a wholly separate institutional cable, in which the cost of the plant is totally chargeable to institutional services, proportional rates could be based on bandwidth used as well as the number of terminals used. If institutional services are provided on a dedicated portion of the regular subscriber network, a workable plan may be to base rates on equipment costs and an amortization period and to set a reasonable internally generated rate of return on investment. A portion of the margin may be allocated to general system support as a simple percentage, without corresponding to frequency of transmission or amount of plant utilized.

Most telephone company tariffs are keyed to plant mileage, but this approach does not seem valid for cable TV institutional systems. A twisted pair connection links every user location directly to a telephone company switching site, while with cable television all of the system is used in each transmission; the system can serve 100 customers as easily as five.

Cable management must chart a careful course in developing dependable, cost-effective services, progressing from general to individually tailored packages as it moves through the "shake-down" period in developing this new technology. Skilled, responsive staff and competitive rates will be two elements necessary for success.

Cable, telephone, and local loops

Because the switched voice system is found in practically every home and office in the country, it will be difficult for cable TV institutional networks to compete with POTS—plain old telephone service. However, many private corporations and public institutions are examining ways in which they can control telecommunications expense, most of which is telephone traffic. Institutional cable bandwidth capabilities can facilitate the development of private telephone systems for both corporate and public entities of scale. In addition, data that travel locally through telephone lines can easily be carried on coaxial cable.

The telephone local distribution network or local loop that connects home and workplace to switching centers was designed to meet the capacity requirements for telephone conversations. Data and voice can now be transmitted over satellite and microwave networks for thousands of miles at extremely high speeds, only to reach a bottleneck in the last mile at either end. Moreover, conventional telephone wires cannot transmit video.

Since the early 1970s, when Federal regulations were eased, many specialized common carriers have developed, using satellite, microwave, and terrestrial links to provide business and data transmission services. The "long-haul carriers" that provide diverse long-distance telecommunications services are becoming well known: MCI Communications, Satellite Business Systems, Southern Pacific Communications, Telenet, Western Union, and Tymnet. Tymshare, Inc., is what is called a value-added carrier: it adds computers to existing transmission links to provide enhanced services to its customers. Applications performed over the Tymnet network include computer timesharing, credit card processing, inventory systems, accounting and statistical analysis, database management, message switching, flight planning, and word processing. MCI, another long-haul carrier, uses a microwave network to provide telephone services. Most of these carriers must depend on telephone company local distribution and thus are limited to low-speed transmission rates of no more than 9,600 bits per second.

The cost of upgrading telephone local loop capacity nationwide will be enormous. It is estimated that local telephone companies will need decades to upgrade to broadband capability. Thus, long-haul common carriers providing data and voice services are seeking alternatives to conventional analog telephone local loops. They wish to secure greater bandwidth and to accommodate high data rates, fast response time, videoconferencing capability, and rapid facsimile transmission. Cable television may provide one local loop alternative.

Institutional networks are coming to be regarded as a potentially efficient component of a multilevel data networking system. The national link is already in place, through 10 domestic satellites. Regional interconnection schemes are still in the planning stages, however; until cable systems are fully interconnected with other regional and national carriers, the institutional network's utility as a data carrier will be limited.

Institutional network design and capacity

Currently, there are three basic institutional network design configurations: dedicated bandwidth on the subscriber ("A") cable, a separate "B" cable that fully or partially parallels the subscriber cable, and a separate cable that passes only a central district of the franchise area, usually the business district. In each case, the institutional network would be capable of sharing certain programming with the "A" cable by redistributing a signal from one cable to another at the headend or a hub when desired. This capacity, however, is usually limited. Placing institutional network services on the "A" or "AA" cable is usually proposed when the subscriber network will be a dual 400 MHz system, capable of carrying 108 video channels. The parallel "B" cable design is much the same, except that a full cable is reserved for institutional uses. The separate "B" cable may be proposed to carry a full 400 MHz or may have less capacity.

Upstream and downstream traffic is "split" between frequencies on the cable. The traditional "mid-split" mode affords greater upstream capacity than the downstream spectrum. The new "high-split" technique allows equal capacity in both directions and is advocated by those who predict that there will be no more traffic in one direction than in another.

The high capacity or bandwidth of a coaxial cable system allows it to carry multiple video signals simultaneously. Television signals require a bandwidth of about 6 MHz, whereas telephone requires only 4 kHz. Digital data signals require significantly less bandwidth. Thus, a cable system can support a variety of two-way signals. Moreover, cable is cheaper to install than conventional wire, and many users can tap the same coax rather than requiring a twisted pair connection from each user terminal to each other's terminal, typical in conventional baseband installations. Coaxial cable is also easier to repair than telephone lines. If a link is cut at any point, repair merely entails splicing one length of cable rather than tracing a fault through numerous pairs of twisted wires.

Institutional network designs have tended to incorporate limited switching capacity on the local level. The ability to route signals from one terminal point to another and to switch video, audio, and data signals to specified channels is critical to a high-traffic network. If there is a high demand for data services, it is not certain whether many of the proposed cable network switching systems will be efficient.

To interface office equipment and computer terminals with the cable network, a building must be wired internally with coaxial cable. Many older public buildings and schools across the Nation have been wired with baseband cable, which has about 50 times less capacity than coaxial cable.[1] This automatically eliminates the capability for teleconferencing, monitoring, and centralized traffic control, because baseband cable cannot handle most of these functions. Buildings wired with baseband cable, therefore, face the relatively expensive prospect of internal rewiring.

Some commercial businesses, including large office buildings, have also been wired with baseband systems, which cannot pass the higher frequencies used over coaxial cable. Thus, these local area networks, or internal wiring systems that connect business machines to each other, cannot hook into the cable system without expensive rewiring.

Planning for utilization

To determine a government's service needs, officials should carry out a needs assessment focusing on:

1. Work objectives
2. Information flows
3. Bottlenecks encountered
4. Projected changes in operation
5. Anticipated future needs
6. Modes of communication employed
7. Types of hardware in use
8. Time and duration of transmissions
9. Present costs for hardware and transmission links.

Officials should also perform a cost/benefit analysis of using broadband cable. Most public institutions use the telephone system as their transmission path for data and voice communications, and most existing equipment has been designed to interface with that system. Therefore, the first step in an analysis might be to determine the savings in telephone line charges, particularly dedicated line charges, if service were shifted to an institutional network.

As institutional networks are activated, public officials can look to cable as a vehicle for such services as electronic mail, facsimile transfer, energy load management, traffic control, and pumping station monitoring. The bottom line will be whether an institutional network can provide the same level of service at a lower cost, or better service at about the same cost.

Policy issues

Several issues are emerging from the arena of the franchising and refranchising processes. One concerns the regulation of institutional networks. In *NARUC II*[2] the FCC attempted to preempt State public utility regulation of cable television. Challenged by the National Association of Regulatory Utility Commissioners, the court ultimately held that the FCC cannot preempt intra-state, point-to-point, nonvideo traffic. Thus, while some aspects of institutional network operations could be regulated by State PUCs—including rates—no States have exercised this option.

As "give-aways" of free channel time and equipment to public institutions have escalated, and as more and more cable companies compete for fewer remaining franchises, there has been a growing recognition that provision of free services to municipalities may constitute a hidden subsidy which impacts on subscriber rates. Hence, many franchising authorities are encouraging the implementation of institutional networks as profit centers, so that revenues from commercial users will subsidize use of the network by public institutions, and subscriber rates will not be affected.

Summary

Plans for institutional networks are receiving increasing attention during evaluations of cable franchise proposals. In evaluating institutional networks, most decisionmakers consider the following elements:

1. Plant mileage and channel capacity
2. Institutions served
3. Capital expenditures
4. Management plan
5. Policies and rates
6. Dedicated terminal and production equipment available from the company to users.

Currently, both public officials and cable operators will find it difficult to make firm commitments on utilizing or developing institutional network services because there is so little actual experience to draw from. However, many institutional networks are scheduled to be activated by the mid-1980s. As businesses, public institutions, and home subscribers become more familiar with data transfer and digital information uses, these networks will have an increasing impact on how we work and communicate in the years ahead.

1.   Baseband signals are transmitted without modification and carry only one signal at a time. Baseband signals (direct current) cannot be sent over lines using amplifiers, as in cable television systems.

2.   *NARUC* v. *FCC*, U.S. Court of Appeals, D.C. Circuit, 1978.

Planning for the Use of Cable in Municipal Services

Fred S. Knight

When someone mentions the word "cable," their eyes seem to take on a funny glimmer. Depending on who is doing the talking, an observer can readily sense the kind of images appearing in the mind's eye of the speaker. Cable operators and owners see a profit potential of significant proportions. Simultaneously, they see encroachment on their access to this profit from "over-zealous" municipal officials, other competitive providers of entertainment services, and, ever present in the background, AT&T. Citizens have visions of 24-hour-per-day news, sports, and movies free of commercial interruptions. Activists see a powerful platform from which they can expound on their positions. Those in the print media (e.g., Time, Inc., the Chicago Tribune Co., Times-Mirror) see a means of keeping up with their technologically mobile subscribers.

In the middle stand the local officials—both elected and appointed—who are responsible for making local franchising and refranchising decisions. When local officials speak about cable, they typically describe an uninviting web of legal, political, and financial entanglements centered on a technology they know little about.

Against the backdrop of these diverse images—and amidst all of the hopes, expectations, and responsibilities—the question of how local governments can utilize cable technology in internal operations and service delivery has received little attention. It is not surprising to find, therefore, that while cable is now being

Reprinted with permission from Management Information Service Reports, vol. 14, no. 6 (Washington, D.C.: International City Management Association, June 1982).

used in municipal operations, the level of utilization is low. But, interest in experimenting with cable utilization by local governments is increasing, and, as the modern cable systems currently under construction come on-line, municipal utilization will rise dramatically.

Cable wars: one path to peace

Cable's growth in recent years has been fantastic:

1. Between 1970 and 1981 the number of cable systems in the United States almost doubled.
2. At the end of March 1982 there were 4,743 systems in more than 13,000 communities.
3. Cable reaches 25 percent of the nation's homes.
4. The penetration rate of cable (i.e., number of homes taking cable vs. number of homes the cable passes) is 40 percent to 60 percent.

But all this growth has not come easily; not to the cable companies nor to the communities. One former president of a major cable company described the cable franchising process in this way: "Cable franchising occurs in an environment where excesses are encouraged and realism is penalized." David Korte, Vice-President of the Cable TV Information Center, puts it like this: "The applicants are promising not only more than what the city wants, but more than they are capable of delivering."[1]

The cable franchising process has become known as the cable wars—a battle that all too often leaves behind an unhealthy residue of mistrust and disrespect. To some extent this hostility is inevitable. The cable company is seeking to minimize its risk and return the maximum profit to its owners and stockholders. Local officials, on the other hand, are seeking to bring as much cable service into the community as possible at the lowest possible price for the citizens. As if these opposing perspectives were not enough to contend with, local politics and the personalities of the protagonists can be expected to further complicate the bargaining process.

There may be an avenue out of this confrontation, or at least an area of sufficient mutual self-interest that will limit future cable wars in both scope and intensity. On October 26-28, 1980, the University of Wisconsin hosted a seminar entitled "Cable and the Cities," that was well attended by both local officials and cable industry representatives. During one of the sessions, an industry official predicted that by the end of the decade, 70 percent of national cable revenues will come from services other than entertainment.

The cable industry thus knows that entertainment services—movies, sports, and even news—represent only the tip of their eventual revenue iceberg. At the same time, local officials are actively seeking out new ways to reduce costs and/or improve their service effectiveness. The application of cable technology to municipal operations thus represents an avenue of exploration where both cable operators and local governments might benefit. That is, local governments will benefit if costs for the cable service do produce actual savings, and if the new cable-based service delivery systems can demonstrate effectiveness, affordability, and reliability. As will be discussed later in this report, the early results in some specific service areas look promising.

Coaxial cable: a transmission medium

If local government officials are going to exploit successfully the potential of cable technology, they need at least a marginal understanding of how it works. Cable is a transmission medium. It is like a highway—perhaps calling it a toll road is more accurate—for transporting voice, video, and data transmissions. What makes cable so special is that it can handle all three types of transmissions with good quality, at high speed, and in large volume.

In order to capitalize on cable technology it is essential that local officials stop thinking about cable "television" systems and start thinking about cable "communication" systems. It is not unlikely that the phrase "cable television" will soon be replaced by "cable communications" in the same way that the "horseless buggy" became known as the "car" and "iceboxes" became "refrigerators." To be sure, cable has a close and enduring relationship to television, but its uses today and for the future go much, much further.

Targets of opportunity

If cable is a communications transmission medium, it seems appropriate for local officials to begin their exploration of cable's potential for their operation in terms that relate to communications. Regrettably, there is no standard or well accepted "communications planning methodology" reliably tested in local governments today. Local officials will have to be eclectic, relying on their common sense, borrowing from traditional planning and management techniques, and looking at other institutions and the private sector for ideas and data.

Fortunately, some work does exist to draw upon. In an article in *Datamation*, Archie McGill, Vice President of Business Marketing for AT&T, gave a clue from the private sector for how to begin when he wrote: "The nub of business communication opportunity lies in understanding that 20 percent to 80 percent of total operating expenses is direct communications expense— phone, meeting, travel, document handling, and associated sala- ries. Much of this is personnel expense dollars."[2]

While no national data on these expenditures by local governments have been systematically collected or analyzed, this author has posed McGill's proposition to about 200 local officials in the past six months. The reaction was that their local governments were probably expending 50 percent of their daily operating dollars on the expense items mentioned by McGill.

Getting a handle on the appropriate management systems and hardware to contain or reduce those costs will not come quickly or easily. Only the largest private companies have had much experience. The Dayton-Hudson Corporation undertook a multi-year communication and information system study of itself in the mid-1970s. While the process was lengthy and the subject complex, the basic methodology is one already familiar to local government officials.

First, an information steering committee was formed con- sisting of senior level Dayton-Hudson management. Under the auspices of this committee, surveys were administered to the affected departments. The survey results were analyzed, con- solidated, and then reviewed by the committee. Then, prelimi- nary recommendations about the new system were developed. At this point the committee went back to the user level to discuss and negotiate its proposed recommendations.

These basic steps—appoint individuals and assign respon- sibility; data collection; data consolidation; data review; prelimi- nary recommendations; and user feedback—are inherent in any sound management planning process. What is different is the application by local officials of these steps to telecommunica- tions in general, and cable in particular, in examining municipal administration and service delivery systems.

Any planning process for cable utilization carried out at the present time should be developed with the following consider- ations:

1. Cable is a transmission medium. It is a delivery system for voice, video, and data communications.
2. Cable is part of—and interacts with each element in—an evolving telecommunications milieu that includes: com- puters—mini's, micros and mainframes; changes in tele- phone rate and service structures; and automated office equipment.
3. There are no standard or "pat" cost-benefit formulas. The work that exists to date is experimental and site-specific.
4. An organization's activities must be thought about from a

telecommunications perspective in order to see how the components of the telecommunications milieu fit together.

Some work has already been done in examining municipal organizations from a telecommunications perspective. In September 1979, then-City Manager George Schrader of Dallas, Texas, sent a memo to the city's department program managers requesting them to "identify potential uses of CATV in delivery of services and departmental administration." Schrader wanted more than just a laundry list of potential uses, so he asked the staff to submit the information in a way that linked potential uses to the pressures the city and each department would face in the next 5 to 10 years. His recommended format for the issues paper is reproduced in Exhibit 1.

I.   **Scenario of the future (5 years and 10 years)**
  a. Description of departmental operations. What's similar? What's changed?
  b. Major issues to be faced
  c. Impact of current trends
   • Energy crisis
   • Inflation
   • Limitations on revenues/resources
   • Demographics
   • Transportation
   • Other

II. **Potential uses of telecommunications**
  a. Survey of existing and currently feasible municipal uses. What could be used when the CATV system is operational (5 years)?
   • Service delivery
   • Administration
   • Regulation
  b. Possible uses (10 year forecast)
   • Service delivery
   • Administration
   • Regulation

III. **Recommendations**
  a. Considerations for franchise
  b. Budget implications
  c. Next step—what process do you recommend to accomplish your recommendations?

Exhibit 1. Format for developing a city department issue paper on telecommunications, Dallas, Texas. (Source: Analysis and Summary: Telecommunications Issue Papers, *Dallas Municipal Library Department, November 1979.)*

I. One Way Cablecasting.
   a. Proceedings of the council and boards.
   b. Interdepartmental training and information: new employee training; new procedure implementation; continuing education.
   c. Client training and education programs: at home workers; new technologies; regulation compliance.
   d. Visual history of city.
   e. Court cases.
   f. Dissemination of information and education to citizens, including: driver training and safety; fire prevention; traffic information; emergency warnings; consumer information; city public relations; and job information.

Problems and considerations in use of one way cablecasting:
   1. Number of facilities and staff needed for production.
   2. Legality of court proceedings.
   3. Location of production facilities.
   4. Portable equipment.

II. Interactive Modes.
   a. Service delivery: client interviewing and screening; problem solving; polls, citizen surveys; information gathering; magistrating of prisoners; paramedic functions.
   b. Administrative: field reports; at home work; technician training; procedural updates, conferences.

Problems and considerations for interactive modes.
   1. Eventual channel allotment may not hold all programs, since some may need to be dedicated channels (i.e., police department, at-home work).
   2. Some programs requiring dedicated channels might not be able to fill a channel; however, compatible programs might share channels.
   3. Paramedic and other fire department uses would require portable equipment.
   4. Many of the service delivery client groups would not have home access to the interactive programs targeted to them.
   5. Public access points would be required for one time interactive use, such as job interviewing.

III. Digital Information (nonvideo).
   a. Meter reading.
   b. Traffic control (could be visual monitor).
   c. Flood control (could be visual monitor).
   d. Energy load management.
   e. Burglar alarm systems.
   f. Fire early warning systems.
   g. Purchase of events tickets.
   h. Computer data interface.

   i. Electronic mail/memoranda transmission.
   j. Electronic funds transfer (fines or city services).
   k. Health monitoring of police and fire personnel.

Problem and considerations in digital information use.
   1. The state of present technology and start up of systems may put this at lower priority level; capability could be built in. Some of these applications require total saturation (reaching every household) to be effective.
   2. Alerting systems required for digital monitoring.

IV. Use of Dedicated Channels.
   a. Aviation and transportation information.
   b. Fire monitoring surveillance.
   c. Security monitoring of city buildings.
   d. Flood and traffic control.
   e. Reserved emergency channel.
   f. Client assessment.
   g. Paramedic use.
   h. Energy load management, and other digital applications.
   i. At home work programs.
   j. Police magistration.

Problems and considerations in use of dedicated channels.
   1. Number of channels needed could be a problem. Compatible programs not able to fill a channel might share time.

V. Visual Monitoring.
   a. Building surveillance.
   b. Neighborhood fire monitoring.
   c. Traffic control.
   d. Flood control.

Problems and considerations in use of visual monitoring.
   1. Amount of equipment needed—initial cost and maintenance.
   2. Constant assurance of system integrity.
   3. Alerting systems required for visual monitoring.

VI. Regional Interconnection.
   a. Regional meetings of municipal officers and special associations.
   b. Regional information.
   c. At-home work programs.
   d. Regional emergency alerts.

Problems and considerations with regional interconnection.
   1. Availability of another franchise in needed areas.
   2. Total saturation for regional emergency alerts.

Table 1. Potential cable uses: city of Dallas analysis.

The format for the issue papers used by Dallas is useful for several reasons. First, it is transferable to virtually any community regardless of size or condition. The kinds of questions asked are not unique to cities of Dallas' size or economic vitality. Second, it assumes change—change in the character of the community, change in the resources available to local government to carry out its operations, and change in the actual processes of municipal service delivery, administration, and regulatory functions. Third, it asks the staff to consider how telecommunications and cable can become woven into the fabric of their departmental activities. Contrast this approach to the way computer technology has been introduced helter-skelter into many municipal organizations. Fourth, while this exercise was undertaken before Dallas' cable franchise was awarded, it could occur prior to franchise renegotiation as well.

In November 1979 the Dallas staff completed an analysis and summary of the issue papers. The results are summarized in Table 1. The Dallas staff decided to organize the potential uses into six categories based on system capabilities: (1) one-way cablecasting; (2) interactive (two-way) modes; (3) digital information (nonvideo); (4) dedicated channels; (5) visual monitoring; and (6) regional interconnections.

This matrix approach to organizing municipal activities is a critically important step in developing a rational telecommunications planning process. Rather than emphasizing municipal departments *per se*, the organization of activities into levels of system design helps the manager develop an overall strategy for deploying the new technology. Moreover, it can help managers plan for the integration of telecommunications in a gradual manner depending upon the outcome of negotiations with the cable company or the entry of new noncable telecommunication vendors into the field. Managers can use this matrix approach to identify high priority targets of opportunity, and more important, to get a sense of how their organization might operate in the future. Rather than approaching telecommunications in a piecemeal fashion, this approach gives the manager a "first cut" at systematically organizing a large number of municipal activities and functions into telecommunications terms. Managers can then proceed with this wider vision on the basis of local community needs, resources, and vendor/cable company availability and reliability.

Institutional networks

During the late 1970s, as cable franchising activity spread, it became apparent to both the cable industry and local officials that municipal organizations had the potential to become significant consumers of cable services. At the same time, technological changes were occurring that allowed for computer-switching from one cable to another. As a result, the concept of an institutional network developed.

The institutional network was originally conceived as a tool principally for the public and nonprofit sector, connecting facilities such as police and fire stations, schools, hospitals, and city/county administration, agencies, and institutions. However, the high costs associated with this type of system has caused the cable industry to become fearful of what an underutilized institutional network could do to the "bottom line." As a result, these networks have recently become more diversified in scope, with the industry seeking to link the concept to the lucrative business communications market.

Cincinnati is one city that is actively planning for utilization of its institutional network. In October 1981 the city hired a telecommunications consulting firm, The Bertman Group, to help identify communications cost savings and capabilities that would involve the institutional network. Cincinnati's franchise to Warner-Amex stipulates only the number of miles and number of channels (upstream and downstream) that the network will have. Connections to the network are to be dropped at city agencies and public facilities—including schools, educational facilities, health facilities, public safety agencies, arts, cultural and recreational organizations, and community and social service agencies. However, the franchise does not address the hardware in the buildings that will be necessary to interface with the network, the costs associated with that hardware, or projected usage. Indeed, at the time the franchise was awarded there was no complete profile of public telecommunications needs.

The consultants began their analysis of Cincinnati's telecommunications activities with a series of introductory meetings with city departmental personnel. In December 1981 a seminar for city staff was held that discussed the historical background of cable TV and institutional and business applications. Samples of the technology were shown to the group, explained, and discussed. Then a questionnaire was administered to city departments that solicited information on the types of telecommunications services the department used, the quantity of circuits and service needed, estimated annual expenditures, and projections of how telecommunications service might change in the future.

To supplement the questionnaire, interviews and small group discussions were held with the departments that were principal telecommunication users. Then the questionnaires were completed and analyzed by the consultants.

It proved difficult to get an actual total for the city's telecommunications costs. Based on the data available to the consultants they estimated the leased telephone bill to be $500,000 per year. The consultants "believe that dedicated phone links can be replaced by using the cable network and interface hardware whose cost can be paid back in 1 to 2½ years. The expected useful life of the equipment is ten years."[3]

The consultants also found that in terms of user requirements, the largest existing use of telecommunications is data communications. Additionally, they found that the services the city's agencies are most interested in adding to their telecommunications capabilities are training and teleconferencing.

A partial list of the study's findings is shown in Table 2. The evidence provides a graphic demonstration about the amount of money expended on data communication and transmission.

Cincinnati is studying the recently submitted consultant

Department	Use	Annual Cost
Finance	Data Transmission/ Alarms	N/A
Health	Data Transmission/ Alarms	$130,000[1]
Municipal Garage	Fuel Usage Control	12,000
Parking Facilities	Traffic Sensors/Alarms	N/A
Police	Data Transmission	N/A
Public Library System	Data Transmission/ Alarms	N/A
Recreation Commission	Burglar/Fire Alarms	5,500
Regional Computer Center	Terminal Interconnect	100,000
Research Evaluation	Data Transmission	15,000
Sewer	Data Transmission/ Telemetry	106,000
Telecommunications	2-way Radio Con./ Alarms	50,000
Traffic Engineering	Traffic/Alarms	Owned
University of Cincinnati	Energy/Alarms	39,000
Medical Library	Security	N/A
Water Works	Data Processing/ Telemetry	20,000

1. Includes modems, lines, terminal leases.

Source: The Bertman Group, Inc. *Institutional Cable Network Study: Final Report*, prepared for the city of Cincinnati, March 1982.

Table 2. Existing communications links and annual cost, Cincinnati, Ohio.

report and assessing how best to proceed. One option under consideration is to select a public building for pilot testing to identify wiring costs, interface equipment reliability and costs, and service impacts.

A number of other communities are planning an institutional network or have made it a part of their franchising agreement. Among them are Dallas and Fort Worth, Texas; Kansas City, Missouri; Northwest Hennepin County and Southwest Hennepin County, Minnesota; Eastern Oakland County, Michigan; Scottsdale, Arizona; and Skokie, Illinois.

As these networks come on line, the infrastructure for the "information age" so long predicted will finally be in place. What lies ahead though for the short term is site-specific experimentation, feasibility testing of new services, and difficult negotiations over who can use the network, for what purposes, at whose liability, and at what cost.

Cable utilization by local governments

Actual cable utilization in municipal operations is just beginning. The modern cable systems negotiated and franchised in the late 1970s are still either under construction or in an experimental service delivery mode. There are, however, a number of communities that are already using cable for a variety of municipal activities.

Overland Park, Kansas, has integrated local traffic light signalization with the local cable system. A centralized computer that regulates the city's 55 major intersections is located in the Overland Park City Hall. The cable lines, which are leased by the city for $5,000 per year, allow the city an inter-connect that would otherwise have to be made via telephone line or municipally-planted line. Cable traffic signalization systems are also under construction in Grand Rapids, Michigan; Paterson, New Jersey; and Arlington County, Virginia.

The Shawnee-Mission School District (representing schools from 10 area cities and towns) broadcasts its educational programming over two local cable channels from 8:30 a.m. to 4:00 p.m. every day during the school year. A total of 1,200 hours are broadcast annually. Programming comes from three major sources: 25 percent of the programs are locally produced, others are rented, and the remainder are recorded off the local public television station. Abiding by the franchise agreement, the area cable company supplied drop lines at all school buildings. Each school classroom is equipped to be hooked to the system, and televisions are moved from room to room depending upon teacher need.

Madison, Wisconsin, has a cable franchise agreement that allows for 3 of the 12 channels to be set aside for community use (an educational channel that is being planned, a community channel, and a government channel). On the government channel, the city cablecasts city council, county board, and school board meetings. With the exception of city council meetings, production for the government channel is done solely by the city. The city council meetings are done in cooperation with the local cable firm to allow for split screening. Also available on the government channel are programs on local news, budget hearings, and job vacancies.

Lexington, Kentucky, is completing its institutional network that will interconnect city departments. The system will also have camera drops at the city's major intersections for traffic monitoring. Hospitals, fire stations, local schools and other public facilities will be able to conduct training programs. The "loop" will also interface with channels on the subscriber loops, creating a high quality communications network.

Brea, California, located 30 miles from Los Angeles, utilizes an internship program to help run the local cable system. California State University at Fullerton, which is known for its excellent communications department, has set up a program whereby students can receive college credit for working with Brea's Telecommunications Division. According to City Manager Wayne Wedin, many of the interns actually stay on voluntarily to gain additional experience after completing their 150 hours of internship. Brea is currently using cable for in-service training, documentaries on city programs and issues, and cablecasts of council meetings.

Seattle, Washington, uses its access channel to create a community forum in the spirit of the New England town meeting. For instance, when a city utility was seeking a rate increase, a 1½-hour program was aired over cable. One concern was that only those homes that had cable would be able to view this important program. To insure access to all citizens, leaflets were circulated indicating that any interested citizen could view the session at a local library. A similar program was aired on the topic of park and recreation policies and plans. Both programs were highly successful.

Tacoma, Washington, has created its own production system and actively uses it. Among other things, they produce public service announcements on installing smoke detectors for the fire department and PSAs on safety ideas for the police department.

These spots are also aired on commercial television. The city also produces 5 to 10 minute weekly programs for its departments. The Tacoma city council chambers have been set up with three cameras, and the Tuesday evening meetings are cablecast throughout the community. Production equipment is also used by the city for diverse purposes such as taping traffic flow in areas that the Department of Public Works is considering for traffic changes. An eight-segment training film was also produced that was used in Tacoma and then circulated to libraries across the country.

Prairie Village, Kansas, has used the local government channel to air a continuous listing of city news and announcements using a character generator. A keyboard is located in the city hall to allow for immediate updates on city information. Also aired on the city channel are municipal arts activities, high school athletics, monthly reports from the mayor, governor, and U.S. congressional representatives. A hotline is operated to facilitate audience participation during these reports. Special programming is also prepared by city departments on such subjects as home weatherproofing and installing smoke detectors.

In **Massilon, Ohio,** the police department is interconnected with the cable system to form an emergency alert network. In the case of an emergency, an officer in the police station can activate an interruptive emergency alert message that will be displayed on the TV screen. A voice message is also transmitted to give information on a specific warning. The system can be used for a warning or evacuation notice and was designed primarily as a tornado watch system. The tornado alert system has been activated at least three times since its installation.

Iowa City, Iowa, has set aside four access channels for government, library, public, and educational use. Live city council meetings, department documentaries, and 24-hour character generation are broadcast over the government channel. From the library, children's story hours are cablecast and promotional spots are given on the library's modern computerized reference catalog. The city hopes eventually to interconnect the library computer with the cable system. This would allow city residents to survey the available books while remaining at home and then "check out" any particular book using their television and touch-tone phone.

Spokane, Washington, operates a government channel five days a week from 9:00 a.m. to 9:00 p.m. They cablecast board and commission meetings as well as training films and public relations segments. There are also educational channels run by a consortium of area grade schools, junior colleges, and colleges. The programming includes weekly informational programs, telecourses, and a tape catalog that is shared by all secondary teachers wishing to use television in the classroom. The city has also concluded an agreement with Eastern Washington University. The university will soon begin assisting in hardware and program development, as well as supply interns to aid in programming.

Reading, Pennsylvania, is the site of a unique, experimental project that uses two-way interruptive cable to encourage citizen participation. The system revolves around neighborhood communications centers (NCCs). Citizens that are hooked up to cable can receive programs and then respond back to the neighborhood communications centers via telephone. The city uses the system as a means of communication between citizens and agencies. The system has been successful in fulfilling its goals of: (1) developing the role of citizens as initiators of programming; (2) using neighborhood facilities as origination sites for programming; (3) developing spontaneous, interactive programs; (4) generating a diversity of public service programming; and (5) serving distinct subgroups of the population (i.e., senior citizens). Sing-alongs, recipe exchanges, and discussions with city officials have combined to increase knowledge about public services and involvement in political processes as well as increase participation in social and community activities.

Lansing, Michigan, operates its own government station aside from a library and educational channel. The city channel programming includes civic programming and city council meetings. For local elections, the city channel airs "Meet the Candidate" segments and carries election results. Election results are sent to a computer on the 10th floor of city hall where the council chambers and city production studio are located. This allows the city to get the election results out ahead of the commercial media.

In the **Manhattan Borough of New York City,** Channel L provides air time to groups that fit into one of three general categories: (1) government; (2) community; and (3) nonprofit cultural. Financing for Channel L comes from a subscriber fee. Channel L is devoted to an interactive format. Viewers, via telephone, may call up and question members of the city council, or any of the forty individuals and groups that are regular users of the channel. The 3½ hours of nightly programming consists of three live phone-in segments and two hour-long shows, with a preproduced, half-hour Community Bulletin Board. Channel L has helped hundreds become involved in the neighborhood and city government.

Rockford, Illinois', fire department was the site of a National Science Foundation-sponsored study of using interactive cable for in-service training. The study, conducted by Michigan State University, found that firefighters that used the interactive system performed better than groups that did not. Madison, Wisconsin, and Brea, California, also use cable for in-service training.

Reading meters   Clinton Township, Michigan; Northfield, Michigan; and Springfield/Brockton, Massachusetts, are undertaking experiments to test the feasibility of reading meters via cable.

In examining the activities of the communities listed above, it is clear that public information functions are the most common current municipal uses for cable with in-service training and control systems (e.g., traffic signalization) beginning to occur more frequently. Eventually, voice and data communications (as in Cincinnati) will come on-line. While reliable cost figures are, at present, difficult to assemble, the communities that are using cable perceive that the quality of their service has improved because of cable use.

Some cost estimates do exist. Grand Rapids will pay the local cable company $30,000 per year for the first 12 years of its cable traffic signalization system that will link sensors at over 240 intersections to a central computer. That annual cost is approximately 20 percent less than the city would spend if it owned the system itself, and even greater annual savings occur when comparing the cable system to the proposal submitted by the local phone company.

As these examples point out, cable clearly has applicability for municipal public information and education, service delivery, and administration. Assessing the cost effectiveness of any particular function, however, still requires a very site-specific analysis. Managers need to examine their service operations from a telecommunications perspective to identify potential targets of opportunity. Then, they must negotiate with their local cable company to design, test, and deliver a service system that meets community needs and community resources.

Conclusion

Cable, as a tool for improving municipal services and administration, is no longer a futurist's dream. While the level of municipal utilization is still low, planning for additional applications is occurring actively in communities of all sizes across the country. While data are still skimpy, there exists a clear trend toward wider experimentation and eventual utilization.

The path of the "Wired Nation," however, is neither direct nor free from obstacles. In many communities the relationship between local officials and the cable company is so bad that creative problem solving and service experiments are simply not feasible at the present time. Proposed changes in federal policy raise doubts about exactly to whom the cable company will need to be responsible. Still another uncertainty involves the intentions of the newly "deregulated" phone system and the role Ma Bell and Baby Bell may play in the provision of services that compete with the cable industry.

To help sort through all these issues the International City Management Association has established a Committee on Telecommunications in Local Government. During 1982 and 1983 the committee will meet with the telecommunications industry, public and private sector users of telecommunications technology, and local officials to explore how telecommunications technologies can become harnessed to improve municipal governance, service delivery, and administration.

While Congress debates and committees analyze cable and related technologies, it is local officials who must initiate the planning and management processes that make sense for their communities. And, together with cable entrepreneurs, they will test the delivery systems that can provide actual service to citizens, reduce costs, and strengthen community cohesiveness. The work is already underway and the instances of municipal cable utilization can be expected to increase soon.

1. Ralph Lee Smith, "Birth of a Wired Nation," *Channels*, April/May 1981 [reprinted as the first article in this book].

2. Archie McGill, *Datamation*, August 1980, p. 94.

3. The Bertman Group, Inc., *Institutional Cable Network Study: Final Report*, prepared for the city of Cincinnati, March 1982, p. 10.

PART 3

Community Programming

A Different Kind
of Television

———————————————————————— Jim Bell

Every Wednesday night at 7:00 P.M. in Frankfort, Kentucky, homes that are hooked up to the Community Service Cable System can tune in and watch the "Senior Citizens Show" on Cable Channel 10. The show is hosted by Viola Brawner, director of the Frankfort Senior Citizens Center, which is undoubtedly one of the best centers in the Commonwealth and probably in the nation.

One day after taping a program, Viola turned to me and said, "I don't know what we would do without you! We get to come in here every week and cut a program on anything we think would be helpful to senior citizens. Then after the show is on TV, if anyone has any questions, they call me at the center. It keeps me in touch with a lot of people we are trying to serve."

"But Viola," I countered, "you only have it half right. Where would we be without you? If there weren't people participating in community television and getting continuous feedback that it was worth the effort, there would be no reason for its existence."

Viola is made for community television. She is completely natural on camera, and her behavior has not been modified by the television process. She knows instinctively that her senior citizen viewers want to see her *as she really is*, and not imitating a broadcast model. She speaks to a specific audience and does not worry about a mass audience. In short, she is very human and comes across that way on television.

People like Viola, who realize these things intuitively, are fairly rare. Most everyone in the culture today has grown up with

———————————————————————————————

Reprinted with permission from *Public Management* magazine, June 1980.

one kind of television, a kind designed to grab your attention and hold it, a slick and quick style, put together cleverly to catch multiple audiences.

Community television is a different *kind* of television, in style, content, intended audience, and equipment used.[1] It emphasizes process rather than product, participation rather than viewing, quality information, examination of the TV environment, and critical viewing skills. In essence, it demystifies the television process and gives people skills to deal with television as a cultural phenomenon.

Community television

Community television means citizens in the community produce programs to be shown on the cable system. In the erstwhile FCC regulation context, the words "community television" can mean programming produced entirely by the cable company (local origination) and/or "public access" or "community access" programming which is produced by folks with no previous television experience.

Since 1972, the words "public access" have acquired a negative connotation among some cable operators who did not appreciate the FCC's mandate for establishment of public access channels in systems with over 3500 subscribers, especially at a time when the economics of providing cable was not favorable. In addition, the concept of public access inspired ill-founded fears among many operators that all of the "crazies" would try to get on TV and spawn interminable problems with censorship and obscenity questions. There was never much objection to the establishment of municipal and educational access channels because of the institutional credibility of those who would control programming. But public access seemed always to be a thorny issue, since the cable company assumed responsibility for programming content, in the absence of having every user sign a warranty and indemnity agreement. Of course the Supreme Court has now disposed of the FCC regulations on access on jurisdictional grounds (*Midwest Video* case), but the negative feelings about the term "public access" remain.

The cable environment in the country today has become a gold rush, with companies scrambling for franchises in the major urban markets. And public access, which was once frowned upon, has become the strawberries and whipped cream served up with the cable company bid, as an extra incentive for cities to award franchises. But the negative overtones of public access linger on, and currently the term "community television" is much more in vogue, with its use implying participation by a broad cross section of the community that on the whole reflects commonly held values.

The Frankfort experience

Community television in Frankfort is coordinated through Cable 10, the programming arm of Community Service Cable Inc.[2] Cable 10 is a community media center that provides a means of expression, communication, and accomplishment of individual and collective goals. As a part of a municipally owned system, we see community television as an ongoing public service to the citizens of Frankfort. Cable 10 focuses on human and spiritual values in our culture and encourages unity and cooperation, the elimination of all forms of prejudice, and the appreciation of diversity. We are concerned with consciousness of the total TV environment and how it affects our daily lives. We are concerned with the integrity and purity of motive of image-makers, as reflected in both the process and the product.

Cable 10 has programming on the system every weekday night, beginning at 7:00 PM and lasting approximately two hours. With a staff of only one person full time and two part time, we obviously depend on community producers to help provide programming.

Some want to do it all, from running camera to editing, while others like to coordinate, interview, host, or get involved in the technical side. A recent sampling of community producers include the executive director of the chamber of commerce, the Franklin County High School Video Club, the director of community relations at Kentucky State University, the county extension agent, the Frankfort Garden Club, Big Brothers-Big Sisters, Elkhorn Junior High School, Hearn Elementary School, Picadilly Pickle Ladies (children's show), the Ron Marlette Sports Network, and a host of individuals. In addition, University of Kentucky interns get credit while working at Cable 10 as producers.

Since 1976 we have carried the city commission meetings live from city hall on second and fourth Mondays. Affectionately called "citcom" by some people, these meetings probably draw the largest consistent audience. On several occasions, viewers have come down to the commission chambers to express their opinion on an issue being discussed. Covering the meetings from beginning to end without editorial comment is consistent with the democratic intent that voters can be informed and understand in a myriad of nonverbal ways the decision-making process of elected representatives. Several city commissioners have said that after conversations with constituents, it was apparent

who had watched Cable 10. These people were well informed on
the issues and the process. The same is true with Franklin
County Fiscal Court meetings which are run on a tape-delay
basis every two weeks. Another important aspect of gavel-to-
gavel coverage is that the traditional media (newspaper, radio,
and commercial television) headline a few items, while community TV can leave the decision of what is or is not important to
the viewer.

Appreciation of diversity

We try to encourage a diversity of programming on Cable 10 and
work to foster an appreciation of individual differences, a
premise consistent with the heterogeneous society envisioned in
the First Amendment but inconsistent with "melting pot" ho-
mogeneity. The classic example is scheduling a show on traditional flower arranging by the Garden Club next to a show on a
bearded fellow who lives in a nontraditional way in the country,
building his own home, shop, and solar shower with incredible
craftsmanship. It is very likely that the people involved in these
two programs would never meet and appreciate each other's
qualities, outside of the context of watching Cable 10. As another
example, we have produced a series of tapes with Kentucky
State University, an institution that was originally a land-grant
school for blacks. One of our purposes in this series was to
encourage understanding and community support in a situation
often fraught with prejudice and misunderstanding.

Process, not product

At Cable 10 we emphasize the quality of participating in the
process of making TV as much, if not more, than the quality of
the TV product. The ends do not justify the means in the
community television environment. Using a portable video camera and recorder to take pictures of yourself and your environment is a way of processing images of who you are and learning
from that feedback. In the same way, community TV is a way of
processing the culture, an electronic mirror feeding back the
values and lifestyles of a community. Television is a language of
forms and styles. Using the tools of TV, i.e., portable videotaping
equipment, helps us learn a new language and begins an ongoing
discovery process about ourselves and our culture. So in many
cases, the actual videotape that was shot may be unimportant
compared to the quality of interaction and the learning that
occurred during the taping process. One probable result is that
people who participate in community TV begin to acquire
critical viewing skills that help them deal with TV as a cultural
phenomenon. As a footnote, however, all this process talk is not

intended as a justification for dull and boring programming, in which producers do not attend to the aesthetics of their images nor the quality of their information.

Narrowcasting

One thing that distinguishes community TV from other kinds of TV is the concept of audience. Cable 10 does not program for a mass audience, but "narrowcasts" for specific audiences. The audience is cumulative over time, so that most anyone can find something interesting to watch at least twice a month. A few community TV operations are now measuring audiences quantitatively, but most of our information comes from program "stars" who get lots of calls from their friends after the show. Another way to gauge audience is the live call-in format which is the forte of community TV. Live call-ins do not happen on other kinds of television. Our most popular call-in was an opinion poll about the color of a historic bridge in Frankfort that had been painted bright blue. What we learned from the show, after the phone rang constantly for two hours, was the willingness of folks to talk about aesthetics in sharp contrast to the general reluctance in a capital city political environment to make known their opinions on more serious issues.

Cable 10 serves as an information and resource center for what some people call "serious makers," or independent film and videomakers. The independents are interested in producing a broadcast-quality product and will spend much more time and effort on a project than an occasional user. The independents are an important part of community TV because they offer expertise and unique perspectives, and their efforts can be supported through distribution networks and post-production facilities.

In the spring of 1980 Cable 10 hosted the central states regional conference for the National Federation of Local Cable Programmers. Since its inception, the NFLCP has been a forum for learning about community TV and its members have worked for healthy community TV situations throughout the country. We are involved in an activity that is still developing, and if people are not plugged into an information network like NFLCP, they tend to reinvent the wheel every week.

A suggested model

Cable 10 is one kind of community TV and should not necessarily be considered as a pattern for operations elsewhere. Every city and town with cable can have community TV, but the way it is structured, funded, and energized will be unique and will depend on the cultural forces in the community. In terms of a model, however, here are a few suggestions. There should be a public access organization that is independent of the cable company, that is recognized by the city council as the official access organization, and that is eligible to receive a portion of the franchise fee to facilitate the citizen participation process in community television. There should also be an entity, a policy board consisting of cable company and public access organization representatives, that has responsibility for the public access channel. The board should be so structured that over a period of time, the access organization assumes primary responsibility for programming the access channel. This arrangement presupposes attitudes of cooperation, flexibility, and adaptability on the part of both the cable company and the public access organization. Without such a spirit of working together, each party becomes entrenched in an adversary context, with little hope of establishing a healthy environment for community television.

The best community TV is organic, on the first floor of Kafka, among the teeming multitudes, changing, alive, and vital. It is an expression of the democratic intent, firmly rooted in the First Amendment and a valuable asset for processing the culture.

1. For equipment buffs, we use Beta ½" cassette, ½" open reel, and ¾" cassette with B/W and color cameras. Black and white is not dead.
2. Community Service Cable is an independent nonprofit management company initially set up (1952) by the Frankfort Electric and Water Plant Board to manage the cable system, with title to remain with the Plant Board. Community Service continues to operate the system under contract with the Plant Board. The major benefits to Frankfort have been an extemely low rate ($3.50/ month) and a publicly owned asset financed solely by user revenues.

Improving Local Community Access Programming

Sue Miller Buske

Initially, we must understand what local community programming is. It can appear in two forms: local origination programming and community access programming. Local origination programming is produced by a staff paid by the cable operator. This programming can be produced locally about activities in the community or it can be packaged programming which is imported and placed on the local origination channel. Further, there is normally advertising placed on the local origination channel which is sold by a local origination sales staff. In other words, local origination programming is produced by the cable operator, is normally expected to produce revenue for the cable operator, and is controlled by the cable operator.

Local community access programming, in contrast, is programming which is produced for, by, and about people within the community. It is generally controlled by the community-at-large.

This article will (1) define the concept of community access to cable television; (2) examine the necessary components to guarantee its success; and (3) suggest ways to improve the quality of programming and the amount of involvement by the community.

We might parallel the concept of access to the print media to the concept of access to the electronic media. In the past the public has had access to the print media and has effectively used it to produce local in-house newspapers, newsletters, and magazines. However, the public has not had access to the electronic media and has not learned how to effectively utilize it. If we look

Reprinted with permission from *Public Management* magazine, June 1980.

at the newsstand, for instance, we see magazines on every interest from photography to economics. Yet, when we look at television as we know it today, we currently have two main choices: broadcast television, which is produced to appeal to the masses; and public television, which is largely instructional and educational in nature. With the addition of cable television we have not only the two basic opportunities of broadcast and public television, but we also have the option of pay programming, movie channels, sports channels, community access channels, and a myriad of other choices.

Let us define broadcasting and narrowcasting. Broadcasting is the type of television which has been most readily available in the past. Broadcasting programming is created to appeal to a large number of people. The concept of narrowcasting is exactly what the name implies—programming for narrow and specific interest groups. Narrowcasting is an alternative which can reflect the diverse interests of the community. With cable television and the availability of local access channels, we now have the ability to narrowcast.

In order to have local community access channels, the city must approach the cable television franchise process understanding the concept of cable as a community resource, understanding that cable is more than just better reception or more channels. It can be a real resource that different segments of the community can effectively utilize. Basic provisions must be provided within the franchise document so that these services can be made available to the community. These provisions include three basic criteria.

1. There must be designated channels for access. In many cases there is at least one channel for public access, one for educational access, and one for municipal access. In some cases it goes far beyond this. Unfortunately, in other cases, there is not even a total channel designated for community access.

2. A basic equipment package is needed which can be effectively used by the public-at-large to produce programs about the community.

3. There must be some provision for an ongoing funding base which will allow community access programming to evolve and happen. Many times a community video access center is started where the equipment is located and which receives basic ongoing funding from a designated portion of the franchise fee to provide training and resources to the community.

For instance, in 1975 six suburban communities in Dayton,

Ohio (Centerville, Kettering, Miamisburg, Moraine, Oakwood, and West Carrollton), joined together during the franchising process in an effort to approach cable as a community resource. These cities negotiated a franchise which offered six community access channels (two each for public, municipal, and educational). In addition, they received an equipment package which provided the basis for a community video center. The cities dedicated nearly 100 percent of the franchise fee to the operation of the Community Video Access Center and the cable regulatory officer who serves the six cities. In addition, these cities formed a multi-jurisdictional organization called the Miami Valley Cable Television Council whose purpose is to foster cooperation and coordinate cable activities. This is only one example of approaching cable as a community resource.

At the community video access center there must be an access facilitator whose responsibility is to train and educate the public (whether that public be city officials, school teachers or community organizations) on how to utilize local community access effectively. The access facilitator plays a key role in the success of community access and local community programming. If that person is not aware of and sensitive to his or her community and how to work within that community, local community programming is bound to be a failure.

The responsibilities of the community access facilitator vary from one situation to the next. The basic responsibilities might include:

1. Teaching basic portapak skills classes, studio production classes, and playback engineering classes;
2. Scheduling equipment use for access users and for these training classes;
3. Scheduling programming for the access channel;
4. Preparing and delivering all program schedules to the local news media;
5. Compiling programming statistics on a monthly basis;
6. Advising access users in preparation of their productions;
7. Developing programs and program series for the access channel;
8. Encouraging local organizations to plan regular or semi-regular programs;
9. Coordinating volunteers; and
10. Contacting and scheduling these volunteers to assist in the various aspects of the access center operations.

One of the first responsibilities that a new community access facilitator must undertake is to develop basic operating rules and procedures for the community access center or the community access channel. Involved in those rules might be a statement of compliance which is signed by individuals who check out equipment and by individuals who wish to place a program on the access channel. That statement of compliance might read as follows:

I have read and am thoroughly familiar with the operating rules and procedures of the public access channel. I am thoroughly familiar with the contents of the program to be taped and state that (1) no advertising material will be cablecast, (2) no obscene nor indecent material will be telecast, and (3) neither lottery nor lottery information will be telecast. I further understand that I assume full responsibility for any disputes arising from my unauthorized use of copyrighted material. I agree to bring all equipment and tape to the access center at the time and date indicated on the above form and to take proper care of all equipment. I assume full responsibility for damage that occurs to equipment and tape due to negligent use. I understand that failure to return equipment or tape on time or in poor condition may prohibit my use of the equipment in the future. I further understand that the access center equipment cannot be used for commercial or money-making purposes.

That statement of compliance would then be signed by the person who checks out equipment or who hands in a tape for cablecast on the access channel.

Other criteria which might be included in the operating rules and procedures are equipment checkout procedures. For instance, any person is eligible to check out equipment once they have (1) taken the equipment course taught by a qualified person and passed the evaluation test given at the conclusion of that course or (2) passed the test related to that equipment's use—this test is utilized to prevent abuse of the equipment, (3) courses would be offered on a regular basis throughout the year and charges for those courses might be set at $5 or $10 with provisions made for those who could not afford the set fee.

Once a person passes the portapak class or test he or she is issued a certified users card (similar to a library card) which is a verification of abilities. This card must be surrendered whenever he or she wishes to check out equipment. The name, address, and telephone number and what the person is qualified to operate is recorded by the access facilitator and kept on file.

Other criteria that might be included in the operating rules and procedures would be: access taping procedures, playback procedures, training classes, a synopsis of each class, records and documentation, and administrative functions.

One of the keys to the success of the access center is a well-operated training program. Training would normally be available in portable video skills and studio production. A suggested procedure for training of portable video skills includes an eight-hour class, provided in four two-hour sessions. The materials covered in this class would include: how to properly operate the portable equipment available; basic camera esthetics; a basic overview of community access across the country; and a thorough discussion of how the individual or group in the training class would utilize the equipment. Studio production classes vary with the sophistication of the studio available to the access user. Normally a studio production class might last from 10 to 20 hours. Other training that might be available would be editing, studio engineering, and studio playback.

Another key to successful community access is community involvement. The access facilitator must organize an outreach project which explains what community access is and how the public can become involved. This outreach can include speaking at the meetings of community organizations with the press, local city officials, and the cable operator. Many times a nonprofit community access organization is formed whose purposes are to foster involvement in community access and to provide both volunteer support and fund-raising support to the community access center. Organizations of this type exist in many communities across the country, including Madison, Wisconsin; Dubuque, Iowa; Kettering, Ohio; Hartford, Connecticut; Austin, Texas; Atlanta, Georgia; and Marin County, California, to name just a few. An organization called the National Federation of Local Cable Programmers (NFLCP) was founded in 1976 to foster the exchange of information about community access and to encourage its development. This organization publishes a quarterly newsletter as well as several other publications, and in addition, it holds regional and national conferences.

In this article we have defined the concept of community access to cable television and have examined the components necessary to guarantee its success. We have also suggested ways to improve the quality of community access programming and the amount of involvement by the community. Basic franchise provisions must be made to insure designated access channels, an equipment package, and ongoing funding. These are key to the existence of community access. The above factors, tied to an experienced access facilitator and a community video center, can nearly always guarantee an informative alternative to broadcast television—community access.

PART 4

Telephone
Systems

System Diagnosis: How to Evaluate Your Telephone System

Paul Daubitz and Robert Ross

This article is designed to assist you in finding out what your present telephone system costs and how well it performs. Diagnosis is naturally the first step in active telephone management. You need to obtain this information before you can make any informed decisions about changing equipment, modifying the telephone habits of your employees, or making any other major change to your system.

Spotting system inadequacies

You can do a very adequate diagnosis by yourself, applying some straightforward, practical techniques described here. You don't need to bring in outside experts or sophisticated equipment, although these resources (described herein) are available to cut down the legwork of diagnosis and can provide fuller insights into how your system is operating. Diagnosis should be an in-house management task.

For any telephone system, there are five basic types of cost cutting opportunities. (1) Unneeded equipment can be eliminated. (2) Equipment with unneeded features can be replaced with less expensive equipment with fewer features. (3) Use of the telephone system can be restricted to priority business. (4) The number of telephone personnel, such as operators, can be cut back. (5) Telephone use can be managed to take advantage of particularly favorable Telco rates. ("Telco" is the standard reference to the telephone company.)

And, there are five basic types of service improvement

Reprinted from *The Public Manager's Phone Book* with permission from Rousmaniere Management Associates, Inc., Hearthstone Plaza, Suite 206, 111 Washington Street, Brookline, Massachusetts 20146.

opportunities. (1) More equipment can be added to handle desired levels of telephone activity. (2) Features can be added to make telephones more versatile and easier to use. (3) Employees can be trained to take fullest advantage of available features. (4) Reliability of service can be improved through maintenance, repair and power failure planning. (5) Monitoring and accounting procedures can improve accountability of users.

One of your tasks in telephone system diagnosis is to identify how you can cut costs and how you can improve service. Another task is to find out how you can capture both savings and better service, or at least strike a desirable balance between meeting these two objectives. A third task is to develop a persuasive plan for taking action.

Assign responsibility   An individual on your staff should be assigned the task of keeping track of telephone system costs and performance. This individual should carry out as complete a diagnosis as possible. It may take several days, but this is the only way for the individual to really understand how your phone system works. Your Telco representative will be available to answer questions as they arise. Later on, you can engage Telco to do a large scale survey (for free) or hire a consultant (for a fee), or install special diagnostic equipment, confident that you can use these resources efficiently.

Diagnosis is an ongoing management task. The individual assigned should budget a few minutes every week (every month for small systems) to review system operations. This enables you to address problems when they occur rather than allow them to fester.

Steps in diagnosis   The purpose of system diagnosis is to measure and evaluate operating costs and performance. To do that you need to:

1. Collect accurate cost information
2. Inventory your equipment
3. Analyze telephone system traffic
4. Analyze employee telephone habits
5. Make a rank-ordered list of opportunities to cut costs and/or improve service.

These diagnostic steps boil down to keeping accurate records, carrying out a few analytical steps, and using the results to formulate an action plan. Keeping accurate records is largely a clerical function. Carrying out analytical steps requires somewhat more talent and resources. You can accomplish a lot simply with paper and pencil.

Telephone professionals have developed mathematical formulas for analyzing traffic patterns and for identifying an efficient configuration of telephone equipment to handle a given level of traffic. Special equipment can be installed to do much of the analysis for you. However, it is worth stressing that you can do a good diagnosis with back of the envelope estimates and common sense.

The most difficult aspect of diagnosis is not recordkeeping or analysis but turning your results into an action plan—in other words, deciding what to do. How much are you willing to cut costs? You may discover an opportunity to pare system costs with a minimum of inconvenience to users and with no negative effects on the quality of service. Sometimes, you can improve service without causing costs to rise. But usually a major cut in costs involves a reduction of service and a major improvement in service results in a rise in costs. You have to use your own managerial judgment in deciding how to compromise between costs and service. There is no absolute standard to indicate if costs are too high for your organization or quality of service too low.

There are a few useful rules of thumb to consider. Some telephone experts believe that telecommunication costs are too high for an average profit-making business if they exceed 1 percent of sales. And some experts believe that service is inadequate if, during the busiest hour of the day, 10 percent of incoming and outgoing calls cannot be completed because the transmission lines, called "trunks," are being used to capacity. Admittedly, these are pretty crude rules of thumb. They don't tell you why your system costs too much, or why it doesn't work in busy periods. You have to do a lot more digging.

The human factor   It is important to bear in mind that telephone system costs and the quality of service are closely related to the nature of your employees' work. Your telephone costs may be high, not because of inefficient use, but because your employees have to use the telephone extensively to carry out their assignments. And, as the cost of making field trips rises with the cost of fuel, it may be in fact more efficient to use the telephone more.

System costs and performance are also heavily influenced by the telephone habits of your employees. Costs may be high and trunks frequently busy simply because your employees make many unnecessary calls. Costs may be low and performance may appear off because your employees don't make calls when in fact they should. Many employees resist changing their telephone habits. As a result, "sure-fire" cost-saving measures may result in havoc, and system improvements that look good on paper are never taken advantage of by the users of the system.

You can arrive at a workable compromise between system cost and performance if you know the nature of your employees' work and their ability to change telephone habits. You can

---

Indicator: Monthly usage charges rising at an alarming rate
Possible Problem: Failure to change telephone operations in response to Telco tariff increases

Indicator: Trouble getting a dial tone for outgoing calls
Possible Problem: Not enough trunks to handle outgoing calls

Indicator: Trouble completing calls once they are dialed
Possible Problem: Equipment failure in your system or with Telco

Indicator: Calls cut off in progress
Possible Problem: Equipment failure in your system or with Telco

Indicator: Complaints of busy signals from people trying to call in
Possible Problem: Not enough trunks to handle incoming calls or busy Telco exchange

Indicator: Difficulties in transferring calls
Possible Problem: Employees not sufficiently trained on use of system

Indicator: Difficulties in communicating between offices
Possible Problem: Failure to use an efficient interoffice system

Indicator: Telephone sets are misallocated throughout the office
Possible Problem: Failure to keep telephone set assignments current with office work patterns

Indicator: Inability to restrict toll or WATS usage
Possible Problem: Poor employee training and supervision

Indicator: Inability to identify who or which telephones originate calls
Possible Problem: No call accounting system

Indicator: "Poor service," including: slow response to repair calls; long waits to get telephones installed, moved or changed; delays in rectifying erroneous/incorrect bills in error; inadequate training and system orientation
Possible Problem: Poorly defined working relationship with Telco or interconnect vendor

---

Exhibit 1. Common indicators of poor, expensive, or inadequate telephone service.

estimate which cost savings measures are practical and which system improvements will be fully utilized. An outside consultant cannot do better than you in judging the human factor in telephone management.

Symptoms of a failing telephone system   Your telephone system may be giving out distress signals that it is in trouble. They may represent easily solved problems or may be symptoms of underlying and more serious problems. Exhibit 1 lists some frequently observed indications of telephone system failure.

Some problems, such as too many busy signals for incoming calls, may be the fault of the telephone company. If Telco's central switching equipment is overloaded, people trying to call in may get an "exchange busy signal" and not a "busy trunk signal." If this is the case, the telephone company is obligated to correct the situation.

It is more likely, however, that telephone problems lie within your system itself. They may be problems caused by malfunctioning or inadequate equipment or problems caused by user habits. Careful diagnosis can determine the true causes of these problems and help you choose the proper corrective action.

Identifying system costs

After you have identified the symptoms of system failure, the next step is to get a grasp of how much the various components of your system cost. Major telephone system cost categories are *equipment* (equipment costs, maintenance costs, and dedicated trunk charges) and *usage* (message unit charges, toll calls, attendant service costs, and diagnostic costs).

The meanings of most of these terms are self-evident; a few are technical terms of the telecommunications trade and need a few words of explanation. A "trunk" is a connection between your telephone system and Telco's network (the term is often used interchangeably with "line"). "Dedicated trunks" are trunks which are used for specific purposes and are generally rented from Telco at a flat monthly rate. Dedicated trunks include local special hook-ups and trunks used exclusively for long distance calling, such as WATS. "Toll calls" include direct dialing calls outside the local area, operator assisted long distance calls, and credit card calls. "Attendant service costs" are the wages and benefits paid to operators standing by the switchboard or other telephone equipment.

Where to collect information   It cannot be overemphasized: the key to any adequate assessment of your telephone system is accurate, detailed, and extensive records. To keep such records, information from widely scattered sources must be obtained. Most of the data on cost appears on your monthly Telco bill. Telco business office records contain more cost information, which can be broken into greater detail.

In general, the records to keep, besides your monthly bills, include memos and invoices for all equipment installed and removed, traffic studies performed by Telco representatives or consultants and surveys of how each telephone set (or station) is used.

Develop an equipment inventory The first step in collecting data about your telephone system is simply a matter of finding out what equipment you already have. The telephone company, of course, maintains a service record of every trunk brought into the installation, and every telephone station where a telephone set can be hooked up and every telephone set. This service record should be updated every time the telephone company installs or removes an item. Unfortunately, this is not always the case. The service person installing or removing a piece of equipment may forget to record every item; and changes may not be properly recorded at the Telco business office. Consequently, at least half the time Telco records are inaccurate.

The telephone company "service charge detail"—the technical name of a service record—is an accounting of all billing for assorted telephone equipment. This form may be designated differently in different localities. In Massachusetts, for example, it is Form 1694; in Colorado, it is Form 2006. The customer may request the service charge detail at any time; however, the telephone company will not provide it without a specific request in writing. If you have hired a telephone consultant, the telephone company will need a letter from you authorizing the release of information about your telephone system to him.

It is very important to stipulate that the information appearing on the service charge detail be translated from standard telephone company language, the so-called Uniform Service Order Code (USOC), to layman's English. Otherwise all you will learn from reading is that you have 3-H9Hs, 10-K44s, a 9DLBP7H, and so forth. Exhibit 2 gives examples of the USOC designation and the English translation. If necessary you can obtain the Uniform Service Order Code Handbook from the commercial supervisor of your local Telco.

Once Telco has responded by sending your service charge detail, you must carefully compare the service record with the equipment you actually have. This is simply a matter of counting your equipment to verify the Telco listing, but in large installations it is not as simple as you might think.

USOC code	Description
CK3 VT	Console
EXB	Night bells
TTN	Touch tone charge for all your trunks and the first 25 stations
KDS	18-button call director
PXA	Main station off the private branch exchange
KV1	10-button telephone
58Z	Station equipped for power failure
S4P	Speakerphone

Exhibit 2. Examples of Uniform Service Order Code (USOC) codes.

First, conduct a spot check. The system is far too complex for you to think you can simply jump right in counting every switch, trunk, and telephone set, but if the spot check discloses serious discrepancies, you should call in Telco to perform a full inventory, in which a "census" is taken of each item. The difference between a service charge detail and a complete inventory is that the service charge detail is a billing record of what Telco believes you have for equipment, and the inventory is an actual count at your site of the equipment rented from Telco that is checked against your service charge detail. Telco provides these services free of charge.

Rectifying the billing for the rented equipment will usually save the customer substantial amounts of money. Some consultants can make a living merely by taking a portion of what their inventory and rectification of billing saves their clients. Even if the full inventory does not save any money, the diagnosis of other problems in your telephone system cannot proceed without an accurate knowledge of what is in the system. For these reasons, the inventory is the logical first step in thinking seriously about your telephone system and service.

Requesting a service charge detail and an inventory of this kind puts Telco on alert that you are questioning the service that it is providing. Watch the Telco response to this request carefully. If it promptly sends you a knowledgeable, concerned representative to find out what you think your telephone problems are, you stand a good change of finding satisfaction with Telco. On the other hand, if Telco's response seems slow and unenthusiastic, you should call that to their attention.

If you are renting interconnected equipment from a private vendor and not from Telco, the invoices for installation of the equipment will furnish the same information.

Summarize equipment and usage costs   You can summarize and report equipment costs on a departmental basis. An example of equipment assigned to a department is a telephone set. Examples of common equipment include trunks and the receptionist's console or switchboard.

The cost of renting, leasing or purchasing telephone equipment is only one part of the total system cost. The other part is the cost of using the system. It is therefore important that the telephone manager keep accurate records of the volume and costs of traffic over the telephone system. Message unit charges are levied by most Telcos for local calls made from organizations. They are described in greater detail below. Toll charges are levied for certain types of calls, such as long distance calls. Like message unit charges, toll charges are variable—that is, they are directly related to your usage of the telephone system.

Total voice communication cost is the sum of all items except for rental and usage of facsimile transmission equipment.

It is useful to compute the cost percentage changes for recent accounting periods, such as month to month, quarter to quarter, and year to year. To do this would simply require adding more vertical columns on the cost summary form. You can thereby find out how different categories of costs have risen or fallen from period to period.

The data included in a system cost summary may be sufficient to give you a sense for cost trends and to help you target management objectives for cost control. But the gross figures are not detailed enough to give information precisely on how costs can be realistically controlled and how services can be improved with minimum financial penalty. The next steps in your diagnosis involve in-depth research on how your system is used and how costs are incurred.

Station review questionnaire   A station review is a survey of how people use their telephones and how they feel about telephone service. Typically, this is done by means of a carefully designed, written questionnaire, although interviews may be appropriate in certain circumstances. A typical questionnaire for the station review is shown in Exhibit 3. This questionnaire is designed to be filled out by each employee at his or her convenience. You may also wish to supplement a written questionnaire with face-to-face interviews.

A station review will not only give you many insights into how your telephone system is performing, it may also generate some immediate improvements. For example, merely carrying out the review makes employees aware of the ways in which they may waste time and create unnecessary telephone usage charges

Dear Staff Member:

We are interested in learning about how you use your telephone and how you feel about your phone service. Please help us by filling out this questionnaire.

1. How often do you use your telephone on a typical day?
   fewer than 5 times --- about 10 times --- more than 10 ---

2. Is telephone contact with people outside your office vital to your job?
   yes --- no, but it is often helpful --- no ---

3. Is telephone contact with people inside your office vital to your job?
   yes --- no, but it is often helpful --- no ---

4. Do you need to make long distance calls?
   5 or 10 times a week --- once or twice a month --- almost never

5. Do you usually receive many calls and make only a few?
   often --- sometimes --- never ---

6. When you are trying to make a call, does it sometimes take a long time for you to get a dial tone?
   often --- sometimes --- rarely ---

7. When people call you, do they complain about having gotten a busy signal?
   often --- sometimes --- rarely ---

8. Would you use a paging system if you had one?
   often --- sometimes --- never ---

9. How would you rate your telephone service?
   excellent --- fair --- poor ---

Exhibit 3. Sample station review questionnaire.

by poor telephone habits. You also may discover that some telephone sets are infrequently used and can be removed. But you should expect that you will receive some requests for more or better equipment.

You can learn a great deal about your system from a careful station review. If your system is very small—less than 25 phones—a station review may be all the diagnosis you need to decide how your system is operating and what to do to improve performance. But with larger systems, the financial stakes are higher, and more detailed quantitative data should be collected.

Analyze message unit charges

Message unit charges are probably the single largest cost item in your summary of system costs; therefore, it is reasonable to analyze these costs first.

Message units are accounting terms defined by Telco and used for billing local calls. Except for a few Telcos that do not use message unit accounting, Telcos charge organizations for their local calls on a message unit basis. (By contrast, households usually pay for local calls through a mixture of flat rates and message units.) The message units consumed in a telephone call depend upon the duration and geographical distance of the call. Telco establishes a charge of so many cents per message unit.

In the Boston area, for example, a single message unit costs 10.57 cents. Calls within a defined geographical distance are charged one message unit for the first 5 minutes and an additional message unit for each succeeding 5 minute period or fraction thereof. Calls within a 2-message unit area are billed 2 message units for each 5 minute period and 1 message unit for each succeeding 3 minutes or fraction thereof.

You should carefully analyze message unit costs in order to (1) determine whether local callers are abusing the system by making too frequent or too lengthy local calls, and (2) determine which numbers and exchanges are dialed most frequently. Then you should take one or both of these courses of action: (1) train users of the system to restrict their use of the telephone for personal calls; and (2) consider installing a flat rate dedicated trunk to reach frequently called numbers or local exchanges, to avoid or reduce message unit charges.

Recording and analyzing message unit costs is always a problem. Telco meters local usage for its own billing purposes, but reports only the aggregate message unit tally at the end of the month for each trunk. Thus, if you have a single trunk for your system, you will be billed by Telco on its monthly bill for an aggregate message unit charge even if you have dozens or hundreds of telephone sets utilizing the trunk. With Centrex and other advanced Telco systems and with systems offered by private interconnect firms a total of message units is usually provided for each trunk or even for each telephone set. (Consider how a hotel keeps track of message unit charges for each room.)

Telco may be able to run an electronic analysis of your message units from their office. They will report to you how many message units you incurred by message unit band and by local exchange. You'll find out, for example, what percentage of your message units are incurred by calls to the downtown exchanges, but you won't find out how many units resulted from calls to specific numbers (other public agencies, "weather," etc.).

Some public sector managers ask their employees to keep

tallies of individual calls for which message units are charged by asking each person using the telephone to keep a log sheet. Each call should be reported on a separate card so that calls can be sorted later according to exchange called. The individual in charge of analyzing these calls can calculate message units from the length of the call and exchange dialed. This manual approach toward diagnosing message unit costs is very time-consuming and will break down if you try to use it on an on-going basis, but you can ask your employees to record a carefully selected sample of calls. This will give you valuable estimates of how your message unit costs are accumulating.

Reliable message unit information is helpful in influencing employee telephone habits. Many office workers believe they have a right to make personal calls during business hours. The widespread assumption that local phone calls are free reinforces this belief. Message unit charges, however, prove that these calls are not free. Some employees may be creating several dollars worth of message unit charges per day.

Even if some personal phoning is acceptable to management, employees should be made aware of the costs incurred. You might encourage employees to ask people at home, such as spouses, relatives and baby sitters, call in on their flat-rate home phones to avoid the message unit expense of calling out from the office.

You can also use reliable message unit information to pinpoint geographical areas within which your system's calls are concentrated. If your office is in virtual non-stop contact with a specific location (such as a central office) or various numbers within another local exchange, you may be able to cut usage costs through rental of a flat rate dedicated trunk.

Telco's diagnostic services

Telco representatives are available to perform a number of diagnostic steps that may be beyond your capacity to do unaided. Telco usually performs these diagnoses without a separate charge—their cost is built into the tariffs. An independent telephone consultant can do these steps for a fee.

If you employ switchboard operators for your system, you may wish to have Telco perform a review of your operators' work habits. Telco can conduct time studies, check the operators' dexterity, use of headsets and habits in making telephone connections. Telco can link an "observing switchboard" to your trunks and count the number of rings before your operator responds to an incoming call, evaluate the quality of response, count the number of rings before a station user responds and evaluate the station user's response.

In the days of manual switchboards, when operators had to

place "jacks" or "pegs" by hand for each connected call, Telco representatives used to evaluate the traffic through a telephone system simply by standing alongside the operators and counting the number of calls. These were called "peg counts." Electronics has come a long way since then. The counting is now done by machine, silently and instantaneously, but the basic principle of traffic studies has not changed.

Telco's electronic devices are designed to record the flow of telephone calls through the system during the day. An informal way of accomplishing this is to count the number of lights illuminated on the console of an office operator every 15 minutes and to simply record this count throughout a few typical days. But these machines are designed to do much more than count completed calls. They can identify all attempted (or "offered") but uncompleted calls, count the duration of calls and report the traffic by volume and destination on an hour by hour basis.

Telco can provide you a computer-generated traffic report on intra- and interstate telephone calls. The computer, having counted all long distance calls made for a month, subtotals the calls by hour of day and destination area. The computer calculates for each destination area the percentage of calls made in each time period. Other long distance diagnoses can report the cost of each call, the exact destination number, and the frequency with which users failed to use a WATS trunk to make their long distance calls.

One very useful Telco diagnosis is the busy study. The purpose of this study is to determine how many attempted (or "offered") calls are not completed in the busiest hours of the day due to the system's trunks being fully utilized. Telco places meters on the trunks to register how often callers receive busy signals. You can ask Telco for a study reporting the total number of times busy signals are received on your system.

The Telco representative will help you interpret the results of a busy study and will recommend any changes to your system which appear warranted. Because telephone traffic on most systems peaks at a certain point during the day, it would be expensive and inefficient to build a telephone system which allows absolutely no delay due to busy trunks. Rather, the Telco representative strikes a compromise, giving maximum service for minimum cost by allowing a probable percentage of calls to find a busy signal during the times of peak usage.

Telephone management systems

Telco does not have a monopoly over electronic, computer-run diagnostic equipment. With the rapid development of computer technology, many private companies are manufacturing this equipment and marketing them as telephone management systems. Some currently marketed systems do more than diagnose your system: they actively manage it.

In the past, only very large telephone systems could afford a telephone management system. But these systems have become relatively inexpensive items, affordable by small and medium sized systems. Some of the basic models are now financially feasible for systems as small as 40 telephones, with monthly expenses of $2,000.

Telephone management systems can reduce costs caused by abuse of the system by 10 to 20 percent, costs caused by misuse 5 to 10 percent, and costs caused by lack of trunk optimization by 10 to 20 percent. The greatest savings with on-site message accounting systems is in the control of local message unit costs— the type of costs that are both very high and very hard to control. These new systems can help to identify employee phone abuse. And they can accurately and efficiently account for costs, extension by extension, a valuable service for local governments and non-profit organizations which must account for costs in many grant and appropriation accounts. Telephone management systems can even indicate when to increase or reduce WATS service and the use of dedicated trunks. Consequently, clerical time devoted to analyzing telephone bills is vastly reduced.

There are basically two types of telephone management systems, known as passive and active. A passive system produces reports which the managers of the telephone system can use in accounting for system costs and monitoring usage.

An active system does everything a passive system does. It records and reports the functioning and use of the telephone system. In addition, however, it actively processes outgoing calls. For example, it will direct all long distance calls to your WATS trunk. In fact, an active system is particularly helpful with dedicated trunks; the active system will maximize dedicated trunk use and minimize message unit and toll charges. An active telephone management system is not cost effective until monthly telephone costs are about $5,000.

Preparing the action plan

We have gone over a number of diagnostic steps—some that you can do unassisted, some that Telco representatives can do for you, and some that an electronic telephone management system can perform for you. Together, all of these steps can help you obtain a practical understanding of how the performance of your present telephone system can be improved to meet your present demands and how you can begin to control costs.

Supposing you have done the diagnosis by yourself, perhaps

with some assistance from Telco and more from salesmen from non-Telco equipment suppliers, or "interconnect firms." You have subsequently discovered a number of opportunities to cut costs and to improve the quality of service and have also found that employees should be given more training and supervision in their use of the telephone system. Your next task is to prepare a plan for action.

As stated at the outset, preparing a plan for action is perhaps the most difficult aspect of telephone system diagnosis. A compromise must be struck between saving money and ensur-

---

TOWN HALL
ANYTOWN, U.S.A.

Recommendations Regarding Existing Telephone System:

1. Remove all multi-button key sets from Accounting and Treasury Department clerical desks.

Station review showed that users of these sets very rarely use the multi-button features. These sets are holdovers from the time when the rooms were occupied by the Mayor's staff. Expected annual equipment rental savings: $2,300.

2. Ask Anytown Telephone Company to do a feasibility study for a dedicated trunk to Capital City.

Analysis of toll charges showed extremely heavy telephone traffic from Town Hall to Capital City. Phone company representative has suggested that we rent a special trunk for a flat fee to handle many of these calls. Expected annual usage savings: $4,000.

3. Conduct a telephone training program for all employees hired since 1/1/78.

Many new employees do not fully understand how to use key sets, how the central switchboard services users, and how they are to report problems with using the telephone. Expected cost savings: cannot be estimated.

4. Ask the Telephone Company to do a feasibility study for a direct inward dialing system (Centrex).

Anytown has never seriously considered going onto a direct inward dialing system. Station review showed that a high percentage (85%) of incoming calls did not require special switchboard assistance and could therefore be dialed directly to the desired party. Green City has recently gone onto Centrex. Expected cost savings cannot be estimated until the phone company conducts a thorough review.

Exhibit 4. Sample memo proposing actions to cut costs and improve service.

ing high quality of service. You must also consider the human factor in telephone systems. Your employees may not accept your cost-cutting measures. Managers often undertake to pare costs by removing telephone sets, only to discover a year later that the amount of sets installed has risen to its original number. Furthermore, managers have installed sophisticated cost accounting equipment to their telephone systems only to find their employees later failing to perform the minimal tasks required to have the equipment function effectively.

Exhibit 4 is an example of an internal memo proposing that certain actions be taken to cut costs and improve service.

Estimate dollar impact Exhibit 5 shows a very practical way of profiling your telephone system's deficiencies, in financial terms that all can understand. It is an annual Loss Exposure Chart, developed and used by the public accounting firm of Price Waterhouse & Co. to estimate the total possible annual dollar loss resulting from a weakness in financial operations. It can be easily applied to telephone system diagnosis.

If you can break down a particular system problem into individually occurring events, quantify the estimated cost of each event, and estimate the frequency of the event, you can use this chart to estimate in dollars the total cost created by the problem for an entire year. Examples follow.

Employee abuse of telephones for personal calls If your diagnosis of the system leads you to believe that about 50 inexcusable local

Est. value of loss ($)[1]	Times per day[2]		
	1	10	50
$15.00	$3,750	$37,500	$187,500
10.00	2,500	25,000	125,000
5.00	1,250	11,250	62,500
2.50	625	6,250	31,250
1.00	250	2,500	12,500
0.50	125	1,250	6,250
0.25	62	620	3,100
0.10	25	250	1,250

Example: A weakness that costs $0.25 per occurrence, and that is expected to occur one time per day, sums up to: 0.25 × 250 days = $62.50.

1. All figures rounded to nearest dollar.
2. Year calculated on 250 working days.

Exhibit 5. Annual loss exposure chart.

personal calls are made daily, and the average length of the calls is 4 minutes, you should then quantify each call into a message unit cost and a cost representing misapplied employee wages and benefits.

Difficulty in getting a dial tone for outgoing calls   If your diagnosis indicates that, on the average day, about 25 calls are postponed for a day or more due to system overloading, you can quantify the minimum cost of so-called lost calls by making a reasonable estimate of employee time consumed in trying to call out. To that estimate should be added a figure representing the cost of delaying the completion of work to be performed over the phone.

The results of the calculation based on the Annual Loss Exposure Chart (cost per event times estimated annual frequency) are a reasonable estimate of the costs, in dollar amounts, created by system overload. The results should be compared with the costs of adding capacity or of reducing the amount of calls.

The Annual Loss Exposure Chart is a handy tool for developing practical estimates of the costs created by particular telephone system problems. Naturally, a great deal of judgment must be exercised in using it. Annual cost estimates derived from the chart are approximate and cost considerations are not exclusive, or even the most important, factors. However, financial impact estimates derived form the Annual Loss Exposure Chart are easy to grasp and communicate.

Management training programs

The first place to call for training on how to manage your telephone system is Telco. Your local company may conduct occasional workshops on aspects of telephone management. If it has not yet run a workshop for public sector organizations, don't hesitate to ask it to do so. Your professional association may be willing to sponsor a workshop and invite Telco representatives to provide the instruction.

The Bell System Customer Education Center provides management training for Telco customers throughout the year. The Center, a division of AT&T Long Lines, conducts a week long course, "designed to equip the attendee with a basic level of knowledge on current voice communications equipment and theory." The Center conducts the course over 20 times a year at either its Cincinnati headquarters or at AT&T locations elsewhere in the country. Anyone with little or no technical knowledge of telephones who has assumed responsibility for managing a medium- to large-sized system would find the course very useful. The Center staff keeps abreast of management training programs run by AT&T-affiliated Telcos, and they can advise you who to talk to within your region of the country.

Contact: Bell System Customer Education Center, 15 West 6th St., 7th Floor, Cincinnati, Ohio 45202, (800) 543-0401 (for calls from within Ohio, call 513-352-7419).

Business Communications Review, one of the leading professional journals in telecommunications, sponsors numerous one- and two-day seminars on telephone management. Titles of seminars have included "How to Select and Implement an Interconnect System" and "Understanding Modern PBX Systems." Instructors include members of the editorial board of the Review. Seminars are held throughout the country.

Contact: Business Communications Review, 36 S. Washington St., Hinsdale, Illinois 60521, (312) 986-1432.

Telecommunications in Your Future: a Manager's Planning Guide

F. L. Smith, Jr.

In the local government manager's never-ending battle to control costs and balance priorities, modern telephone and telecommunciations technology is playing an increasing role. The challenge for the manager is to balance the diverse needs of the community and set a framework for action. But often these needs are in conflict, and the costs of fulfilling them are high. Modern telephone systems can help the manager resolve the conflicts. Equally important, they can help control costs and provide better government service at the same time.

For example, Plymouth, Michigan (population 10,000), found itself charged with expanding its police responsibilities. The Plymouth police department had been covering the two square miles of the city. It now had to assume patrol duties for the surrounding Plymouth Township—eighteen square miles. It seemed inevitable that to cover the outlying police station and to provide the larger area with a high level of police service, the city would have to add to its staff at least a dispatcher and perhaps other personnel.

But, in fact, the obvious solution of more manpower was not the best solution, as the city discovered. The real answer lay in advanced technology. The city had been planning for a new telecommunications system, and in the course of a careful analysis of its information flow, the city found that what had seemed like a manpower problem was actually a communications problem. It was not physical coverage that needed to be increased, but accessibility. By installing a telecommunications system that automatically forwards calls and lets others pick up calls for an officer temporarily out of the office, the city made it possible for police to patrol the area and still respond quickly to requests for assistance without a new dispatcher.

One result was the saving of over $100,000 per year in projected additional expenses. Another was improved service. After-hours calls to local stations could be automatically routed to the central police station. For the first time Plymouth Township had the same twenty-four-hour coverage as Plymouth City.

Plymouth is just one of many cities, large and small, that have benefited from the new communications technology. East Hartford, Connecticut (population 60,000), found that a new system would allow it to handle fire calls more effectively, without adding a dispatcher, by taking the burden of administrative calls off the current staff. It also helped the tax assessor's office handle a heavier volume of calls without adding personnel. Shreveport, Louisiana (population 350,000), has planned for a new system that allows departments and offices, including the municipal library and airport, to be linked for increased efficiency and cost savings.

New tools and new plans

A modern telephone system provided an appropriate, fiscally responsible, and service-oriented answer to Plymouth's problem. On the surface, it seems like a simple solution, but a great deal of technical sophistication lies behind it. Not long ago this solution was simply unavailable. We have moved from the days of clattering manual typewriters, ink-blotted account ledgers, and busy operators sitting at a bank of plug-and-cord telephone boards to an era of word processors, computerized billing systems, and electronic communications.

Today's telephone technology and the evolution of the telephone into advanced communications systems provides a base for new solutions to problems in municipal administration. The managerial mandate today is to replace slow, labor-intensive, redundant, and error-prone manual processes with tools of greater speed, efficiency, cost-effectiveness, and accuracy. These tools provide a variety of new solutions to the problems of providing quality service and increasing efficiency in the office and administrative environment.

Careful study went into choosing the appropriate solution in each example cited above. Selecting the proper tools requires planning. The experience of Plymouth does more than demonstrate the gains made possible by new technology. It also typifies the process by which a successful solution was found:

1. Setting goals (one of which was providing additional police coverage)
2. Analyzing cost centers (including manpower requirements) to discover where the greatest impact is possible

3. Effecting a systems study of those areas to define needs and find viable solutions (in this case, a telecommunications solution).

These are the basic steps of the planning process that lets a local government manager identify the proper approaches, whether telecommunications, data processing, office automation, or organizational change.

But you cannot plan for or manage a technology without some perspective on the features and options it provides and how they might help you manage your services and costs. The following sections outline the importance of telecommunications in local government and track the growth of the technology to illustrate the capabilities it has gained over the past few years.

Telecommunications and information

Telecommunications is a central solution for government offices. It is central because it deals with the communication and processing of information, and governments run on information. Government services are timely and relevant only if they address the current needs of their citizens. Telecommunications provides current information about those needs.

For instance, a government's budget process depends on tight control over revenues and expenditures. Up-to-date information on income and expenses must be readily available. Telecommunications, coupled with data processing systems, can provide this accessibility. Government also must look to improved efficiency in its services to keep costs in line and citizens satisfied. In order for police and fire services to respond quickly, instant access to an officer or dispatcher is required.

Communications, information, and information management, so crucial to tax assessments, response to citizen emergencies, purchasing, billing and accounting procedures, energy control, facility use, security, and other everyday and long-range concerns, all fall within the purview of today's modern telephone systems. Efficient communication of information internally (among offices, between machines) and externally (between government and citizens) makes a big difference in government productivity.

One practical example is fire emergencies. The first minute of response time is crucial. Telecommunications can do more than get the alarm in. It can make sure the alarm is routed to the right station and the right personnel. It can also give the fire department instant access to information about the equipment likely to be needed. In one system currently available, a fire dispatcher has instant electronic access to data on addresses, types of buildings, location of hydrants, and other pertinent information, all stored in a data unit. This is much faster, and can provide more complete information, than the old-fashioned manual index card system. It is telecommunications working.

In short, there is a convergence of functions, and thus a convergence of solutions. Telecommunications has advanced to help meet these needs, and has done so at an astonishing rate.

History

A brief history of recent developments will show how this technology has developed and why local officials must not only plan to take advantage of its current capabilities but consider its potential for the future.

Not long ago an operator handled most of the telephone calls that came into an office and performed a number of valuable functions: message taker, information directory, dispatcher, call router, and schedule keeper, as well as accountant's assistant for long-distance charges. But, as the demand for rapid communications increased, this labor-intensive method no longer made economic or administrative sense.

The problem was not to replace operator functions, but to manage them—and a multitude of others that were emerging—more efficiently, more quickly, and at reasonable cost. The answer was the PBX-based telecommunications system.

First electromechanical, and then electronic, PBXs appeared—and they developed with blinding speed. For example, the Bell System's first computerized DIMENSION® PBX, which appeared in 1975, handled up to 400 lines and provided such features as direct inward dialing so callers could reach an office without going through the switchboard. There were 50 features in all.

Since then, 12 new feature packages for the DIMENSION PBX have been introduced, with the total number of features reaching 150. PBXs are now available in configurations from under 100 lines to nearly 25,000 lines, provided by several PBXs working together in the Distributed Communications System. These systems can provide high-speed data switching, customer reconfiguration of telephones and features in the event of an office move or change in responsibility, call forwarding, automatic call-back, least expensive route selection for long-distance calls, message center service, conference calling, electronic direc-

---

DIMENSION is a registered trademark of AT&T.

tory service, automatic answering and call distribution, and more—or less, if an organization doesn't need all these features.

And progress continues. New systems for smaller users (60 to 100 lines) are now available with over 100 features and options.

The new technology lets the manager solve problems that have plagued offices for decades. It gives better control over operations, in ways that range from more accurate billing of long-distance calls to the control of phone abuse. To give a simple example, an employee of a northeastern city had been making overseas phone calls to family members every Friday afternoon for months. The manager was able to stop this abuse by utilizing the automatic identified outward dialing feature to find the phone from which the calls originated.

Productivity can be addressed through conference calling, which lets the limited personnel of small cities, or widely scattered personnel in large organizations, meet without leaving their desks. Citizens who reach the wrong official can be transferred in seconds, without having to wait for a switchboard attendant. The busy manager can have a phone redial a busy internal number automatically, indicating when the connection has been made.

Energy control and security functions also are possible through new telecommunications systems. Heating and air conditioning can be controlled in buildings. In New Orleans a telephone system turns off the water fountains in public parks. And, of course, in larger installations the functions of message-taking and directory service can be shifted from a secretary to an automated message center.

Moreover, the technology is still advancing. Innovations include:

1. New centralized message desk features
2. Improved data handling capabilities
3. Larger—and smaller—systems at economical prices
4. Network services, which allow dissimilar data devices to communicate with each other for transfer of documents, direct purchasing, interactive file updating, and other purposes.

These all point the way to a future in which telecommunications will play an ever larger role in the management, processing, and transmission of information.

The future of telecommunications is going to be a continuation of its recent history. Likely advances in the near future are:

1. Systems capable of word processing, document distribution, and remote monitoring and control

2.   Systems with data processing capabilities, permitting the entry, updating, and processing of forms
3.   Systems that interface with high-speed data terminals
4.   Systems that provide speed and protocol conversion, permitting the transmission of data and documents between dissimilar terminals
5.   Systems that interface with local data networks, such as Ethernet, Wangnet, and CATV systems.

Making decisions in today's world is difficult. In the future, when even more options will be available, the unprepared manager may be unable to make a wise decision among vendors, all of whom claim to offer the customer the "best buy." The prudent course for the local government manager is to start *now* to develop a rationale for dealing with this environment.

Planning for needs

As noted earlier, the information management planning process involves three steps: setting goals, analyzing cost centers to find areas where the biggest payoff can be expected, and doing a systems study of those areas to define needs and identify solutions.

To show how these rather abstract and theoretical principles have been put into practice, let's look at two of the cases mentioned earlier—East Hartford, Connecticut, and Plymouth, Michigan—to see how they planned for the present (and the future) and the benefits they derived. Each of these cities' goals and needs were very different, and their respective governments found solutions that precisely satisfied those needs.

As a small city, Plymouth wanted to upgrade services and improve efficiency while keeping costs in line and providing for future expandability. With that goal in mind, the city government was able to identify several areas that needed improvement. Interbuilding communication needed to be improved so that the court, the city offices, the police, and the accounting and treasury departments could exchange information efficiently. The city wanted to maintain its close cooperation with two other municipalities in the area, but this required extensive communication, and phone costs were rising. Finally, there was the problem of police coverage mentioned earlier.

The telecommunications solutions selected in Plymouth include tie lines between buildings and between Plymouth and the neighboring communities. This gives easier access at a fixed price, improving efficiency and controlling costs. Since the government staff is small, it must be mobile. Call forwarding lets staff members leave their desks without sacrificing the good communications that are necessary in a small municipality. Conferencing also facilitates the quick resolution of problems by allowing consultation without having to schedule meetings. In addition, the system is capable of data communications as well as voice communications, so the city is ready for the future, when its data processing needs expand.

In contrast, East Hartford focused on two primary goals: to improve services to citizens and to effect dollar savings.

After analyzing its cost centers, the city decided that it did not need all the advanced features that were available. For instance, the government was not interested in a customer management capability that would allow it to make changes in the system internally. It felt it was more cost-efficient to have the vendor handle any telephone moves or number changes. What East Hartford did need was certain features that would let it perform current tasks with greater efficiency. Since the emphasis was on service, particularly to senior citizens, who make up a large part of the population, the government analyzed areas in which service could be improved.

One major problem was an inefficient call-back system. With the old system, when a citizen requested information or reached the wrong number, the call could not be held or easily transferred. Therefore the city selected call hold to let city employees put the party on hold while they got the information. Call transfer capabilities allow staff to forward calls directly to the right department.

The goal of cost containment was addressed through contracting for a stabilized rate, thus avoiding rate changes, and by adding toll restriction to control long-distance calls. As mentioned earlier, the East Hartford system eliminated the need for an additional fire dispatcher and extra staff in the assessor's office, thereby reducing projected costs, while at the same time improving the responsiveness of these two functional branches of the government.

Organizational and technological concerns

For the local government manager, aware of the power of a new telecommunications technology to make the labor-intensive functions of government more efficient, the planning and implementation of new solutions raises a number of questions. Managers are now asking themselves how they can plan and implement new cost-effective solutions that:

1. Can be easily administered and managed
2. Provide improved service to citizens
3. Take into account the welfare of employees
4. Offer minimal risk of disruption to operations if something goes wrong

5. Can lead to implementing even better, newer, more cost-effective solutions if everything goes right
6. Are affordable in today's fiscal environment.

In short, the key concerns for managers are cost-effectiveness, service, employee considerations, minimization of risk, growth potential, and affordability.

Cost-effectiveness In the case of the Plymouth police department, cost-effectiveness was addressed directly, with resulting savings of $100,000 or more. East Hartford saved on personnel costs. But the case of Shreveport shows that savings may not be so clear-cut.

Shreveport chose a system consisting of one DIMENSION 2000 PBX, one DIMENSION Prelude, and seven Horizon® communication systems suitable to the size of the city, with features that addressed its particular needs. There were dollar savings, of course, but the city has found significant savings through increased productivity, even though they are not as apparent as the reduced need for staffing.

By analyzing the time the system would save each employee in the performance of routine tasks, those involved in the planning process projected a total productivity increase over the course of the year. For example, response to inquiries can be speeded by call hold, call forwarding, and conference call features. Automatic call-back lets staff work while the telephone keeps trying a busy number. The time savings may seem small—fractions of a minute per call—but when multiplied by the number of calls per day, month, and year, the additional time available for productive work can be substantial. Shreveport's finance officer actually converted the projected percentage of time saved into wage dollars to find out what additional resources might be available as a result of the new system. This is somewhat speculative, but it helps quantify the productivity gains.

Shreveport also looked at the dollar savings to be realized by administering the system on its own. The inclusion of a customer administrative control system (CACS) allowed the city to handle office moves, the addition and deletion of features on internal lines, and other alterations without service calls. Simple in-house reprogramming through the CACS is expected to save the city $20,000 in change charges each year.

Further dollar savings come from unifying the system so that departments located around the city pay flat charges for tie-lines, rather than per-call rates for interdepartmental communications. This approach is similar to that in Plymouth.

Though these three cities clearly show how telecommunica-

Horizon is a registered trademark of AT&T.

tions can improve cost-efficiency, they by no means exhaust the potential applications of the technology. Another striking example of increased productivity is a county sheriff's department in the Southeast. With three substations located many miles from each other, the officers were finding their manual record transfer system increasingly slow, time-consuming, and error-prone. They used index cards to record complaints, arrests, and so forth. There were 1.5 million cards on file, and they had a 35 percent redundancy rate. Since it took one minute to prepare each card and 1.5 minutes to retrieve it from files, officers were spending the equivalent of 8½ weeks filing and 13 weeks searching files each year.

A phone-based data retrieval and communications system reduced the time per transaction to between 3½ and 14 seconds, for an average net savings of 12 working weeks per year. This alone pays for approximately one-half the yearly cost of the system. The department found that the rest of the cost was more than justified by other advantages—the ready availability of updated data, the increased speed of transfer, and the improved accuracy and reduced redundancy of the records.

Service   Telecommunications technology obviously has an impact on productivity and cost-effectiveness. But what of the second concern of the government manager—service?

Any telecommunications system should be perceived as making government more responsive to citizen needs, whether through faster response times to fire calls, easier access to officials, or more accurate and equitable tax bills. Direct inward dialing to officials, used by many municipalities, is a basic approach, but the new technology can provide other services as well.

For example, while tax assessment is a vital function for local government, the cost of assessment is rising, and in some locales, collections are declining. In one local government in South Carolina, a telecommunications-based data retrieval system has made updating assessments and uncovering overdue accounts more efficient and accurate—and at a reduced cost. Citizens concerned about their appraisals also get answers faster when all the information is on-line.

Communities across the country have found that a simple system for automated jury selection can improve relations with the public. Citizens often are tied up for days waiting for a call that never comes to serve on a jury. The city pays them, even if they do not serve, then sends them home. This builds resentment and doubts about the efficiency of government. By the simple expedient of assigning jurors numbers, then letting them call a telephone answering device in the morning and afternoon to see if their numbers have been assigned duty, the government can eliminate most of the waste of time. The result is real dollar savings for the government and for the employers of the jurors and a saving of time and frustration for the jurors themselves.

Employee considerations   This and the other managerial concerns are more closely related to policy than to technology. Any new system should be user friendly, easily administered, and minimally disruptive of operations during the start-up period. The manager must also be concerned with the dislocation, reassignment, and retraining of people affected by the new system.

Minimization of risk   The system should expose the manager and the government to minimal risk. It must offer (1) reasonable assurance of performance to expectations, providing the expected benefits to the organization; (2) vendor reliability, ensuring that the required maintenance will be provided when necessary; and (3) financial protection, making it feasible to move to a more cost-effective solution if new products introduced shortly after acquisition of the selected system make it obsolete.

Growth potential   The system should have the capacity to move into more advanced applications, and the vendor should have the capacity to provide them.

Affordability   The cost of the proposed system must be within reason for the size of the community. Is the system to be purchased through the use of capital funds, a financial lease, or an installment payment plan in which the risk of ownership rests with the user? Or is it to be acquired through an operational lease or service agreement where the risk of ownership resides with the lessor?

Each of these issues puts the focus where it belongs: on the needs of the organization. In order to plan for the future, you must know your own needs.

With one exception—the question of obsolescence—technology does not play much of a role in this list of issues. The reason is simple: You cannot prepare against technological obsolescence. As sure as death and taxes, any equipment you buy will become obsolete technologically. The issue is how to manage so that obsolescence has the least possible impact on the organization.

Many managers believe that buying new technology is good

planning in and of itself. But any decision-making process that does not focus first on internal functional needs and cost-effectiveness is unlikely to result in the most effective tools for organizational administration. Today's solutions should address today's problems and permit an easy transition to new technology when it is needed. Just because a system uses the latest technology is no assurance that it either does what you want today or will do what you want tomorrow.

A planning primer

The first step in the process of planning for telecommunications is for you, as the manager, to develop a set of primary written goals for the municipality for the next two to five years.

These goals provide a framework for ongoing decision-making, not only for implementing telephone and telecommunications systems, but for resolving a wide range of government issues. Without these goals, individual department managers will make decisions that work at cross purposes with each other and perhaps even affect the long-term viability of the municipality.

Since goals describe where you want to be at the end of the planning period, they should have several characteristics.

1. They should be clear and concise; otherwise they will be open to a variety of interpretations.
2. They should be realistic. Setting impossible goals leads to failure and pessimism.
3. They should aim at a quantifiable, measurable end. Nebulous aims promote questionable achievements.
4. Their outcome should be within the manager's control.

Goal-setting gives you an overview of the government as a total system. It lets you see the relationships among the goals and then to plan total administrative, financial, and communications systems to achieve these ends efficiently, instead of adopting a fragmented, piecemeal, and ultimately less effective approach.

Once the most important goals have been identified, you will know where to concentrate the resources of a new system. A list of goals, arranged in order of priority, is an important tool in allocating resources, whether they be managerial, financial, or technological.

From the list of goals you may determine that the municipality will benefit from an advanced telecommunications system. A budget analysis can help you plan such a system. Your budget analysis will reveal that the major cost centers are personnel, travel, energy, buildings, and supplies. Virtually all of these revolve around information and its communication. Since the elements of communication include face-to-face meetings, document preparation, data, postage, and even travel, virtually every one of these cost centers can be made more cost-efficient with better communications. Teleconferencing, energy control, and other telecommunications applications provide the medium for such improved communications.

The choice then becomes where to invest your telecommunications resources. Again, your budget analysis will help you see where improvements can be made, develop alternative plans, and select the best alternative. On the basis of this analysis, you can draw a simple pie chart to see where you are currently spending money, then judge for yourself which areas are getting more or less investment than they need.

The next step is a systems study analysis. Analyzing your information needs means studying the way information flows through your organization. Your plan will be effective only if you take into account all modes of communication—on paper, by voice, in the form of data, and sensor-based input. Information processing—text preparation and editing, message transmission, document distribution—should also be analyzed. In some cases you may be able to find ways to speed up the flow, or improve its accuracy, by rearranging the current mode or substituting one of the others.

The analysis will identify the input and ask pertinent questions.

1. What is the form of the input (voice, paper, etc.)?
2. What is its format, and is it easy to use?
3. What is its frequency (by the hour, day, etc.)?
4. How does it get there and what does it cost to prepare and transmit?
5. Is it timely and accurate?

The processing of the input, its storage, and the organizational response or output will also be included in the analysis. This should make the interlocking nature of the organization clear and point up areas where improvements can be made in the formation flow.

Ultimately, the analysis leads to the design of a system that meets as many of your needs as possible in a cost-efficient way. This system will not only have the capacity to handle the communications volume you have today; it will be planned for additional capabilities, including increased capacity and expanded features.

Sometimes the best way to plan is to get outside help, either an independent consultant or a vendor representative—or both!

You know what your needs are, but information-management experts will know more about the latest solutions. They may see ways of improving productivity that others would not think of, and they can conduct surveys to help you pinpoint problem areas.

Planning for today and tomorrow

Once all the study reports are in hand from your analysis and/or that of consultants, you can make your decision. You will be able to choose your new system with specific features based on complete information:

1. How the system will improve local government productivity and efficiency, including station by station analysis, the effects on information flow, and the routing of information and communication
2. The impact on your budget, including the cost of the system and cost benefits derived from its use
3. The potential for future expansion to meet growing needs
4. The management of the risk to which the organization is exposed
5. How the new system will improve operations, including how it will affect your personnel.

The result will be an informed choice among the available options.

Planning for the future of your information management system will require thought, work, and time. But it will pay off in the long run in increased cost-effectiveness, improved productivity, and better service—the mandates of the local government manager.

Choice or Chance: Managing Procurement for Telephone Systems

─────── Bill Henderson and Randy Young

Deregulation and changing technology in the telephone industry are creating opportunities for local government managers to reexamine communications systems. You know you will have a choice, but will you be taking a chance? Budget constraints and the need to maintain public services compel the manager to analyze the choices carefully and thoroughly. You cannot afford to rely on unsubstantiated claims about system costs and performance. Rather, you need specific procedures to obtain and analyze the complex technical and financial data that are essential for intelligent procurement. This article is designed to help local governments that are contemplating a change in their telephone systems by presenting guidelines for systematic procurement.

For the purposes of this article, "telephone" is a shorthand expression that encompasses a wide variety of telecommunications systems and features. First, "telephone" means the voice communication instrument you use to talk to a person who is not in the same room with you. "Telephone" also includes the support network of cables, switches, terminals, and computers that sustain the voice communication instruments. Modern telephone systems also include features for conference calls, simultaneous voice and picture communication, and sensor networks for security control and/or energy management. The term "telephone," as used in this article, also includes systems for communicating text and data, such as work stations in "paperless offices," and most data processing and word processing systems. The procurement process described below applies to any of these telephone systems.

Telephone procurement has three phases—planning, solicitation, and selection—which are described below. By following these steps, you can minimize the chance of making an ill-considered choice of telephone systems.

Planning

The planning phase involves selecting a procurement team, defining user requirements, and developing specifications. The specifications (functional, cost, vendor, and general) will constitute the core of the RFP, and they will provide benchmarks for evaluation during the selection phase.

Staff and schedule As manager you should appoint a procurement team that includes representatives of major user agencies and representatives of the following staff functions: telecommunications, information processing, purchasing, finance, and legal. The team should be responsible for all subsequent steps in the procurement process. Naturally, the team may turn to other individuals or committees to accomplish steps that require special skills.

At the same time, establish a master schedule with specific deadlines for each step. The amount of time required will depend on the size of the organization, the complexity of the system, and the availability of team members. The process will normally take five to nine months (see Figure 1).

The telephone procurement process can be conducted at no cost (other than paper and postage for RFPs and communications costs for checking vendor references). If you need assistance in developing user requirements and functional/technical specifications, you will find that some vendors provide those services at no cost, and with no guarantee that they will receive

Activity	Days Required
Planning	
Prepare user requirements	30–60
Establish specifications	30–60
Solicitation	
Prepare and issue RFP, conduct bidders' conference	15–20
Vendors prepare proposals	30–45
Selection	
Screening proposals	30–45
Select vendor and negotiate contract	15–45
Total	150–275

Figure 1. Timetable for telephone procurement.

the contract. If a local government lacks specific skills in technical systems analysis or investment cost analysis, it may contract for such skills from independent sources at modest cost.

Functional and technical specifications   The functional and technical specifications will be included in the RFP to explain your operating environment, service levels, and performance requirements. The functional specifications are derived from the user requirements and should include:

1. Major functions of your organization
2. Approximate volume of transactions (peak, average, and minimum)
3. The physical layout of sites to be served by the system
4. Current and projected size of your organization
5. Special requirements, such as security, redundancy, hours of operation, interfaces with other systems, response time, excess capacity, and/or quality standards
6. Any planned changes in functions and/or site locations that might affect the system.

Technical specifications should be limited to factors that you cannot or should not change, such as climatic and environmental conditions, types of power sources, and zoning/building requirements. Other technical specifications may set standards for durability, useful life, and operating characteristics. The technical specifications should *not* detail the physical or mechanical/electronic characteristics of instruments, terminals, switches, or cables. These are engineering problems that each vendor will resolve in accordance with the capabilities of its product. The more you constrain the technical solution of your functional needs, the less competition and innovation you will get.[1]

Cost analysis specifications   The cost analysis specifications should appear in the RFP as a list of cost elements that vendors must itemize, or they must certify that such costs are included in the charges for basic equipment or system maintenance. A comprehensive cost analysis should include the following, either itemized or "inclusive":

1. Preinstallation costs
   a. Consulting
   b. Design and/or engineering
2. Equipment costs
   a. Operating equipment (including initial system, additional equipment for expansion, and redundant systems equipment)

      b.   Inventory (spare or replacement parts)
3. Installation costs
      a.   Site preparation
      b.   Cable or cable replacement
      c.   Shipping charges
      d.   Installation (initial system and any planned expansion)
      e.   Initial training (of users, "attendants," and in-house system maintenance personnel)
4. Operating costs
      a.   Operating supplies
      b.   Insurance
      c.   Equipment maintenance (other than inventory and in-house maintenance personnel)
      d.   Network charges by regulated entities (i.e., network access, private line, off-premise extensions)
      e.   Facilities operations (i.e., floor space, power/utilities)
      f.   Training for new employees (not initial training of existing employees; you will need to predict turnover rate)
      g.   Administration
5. Special costs
      a.   Cost of capital (only applies if system is "financed")
      b.   Removal charges (when or if system is replaced)
      c.   Salvage value (expressed as a negative cost; applies only to purchased systems)
6. Analytical data
      a.   Useful life (you may specify useful life to ensure comparability of cost analyses)
      b.   Number of personnel (attendants, maintenance, etc.) employed by your organization to operate the system.

You should require vendors to identify any items that are to be provided by you so that you can estimate those costs as part of cost analysis during the selection phase.

Costs should be presented in a multiyear format that approximates the useful life of the system (five to ten years).

Figure 2 is an example of the cost analysis format for a telephone RFP. The multiyear approach accommodates several factors:

1. Vendors who lease their systems can list the annual lease charges (including anticipated rate changes) over the useful life of the system. The total cost of these charges can be compared to the purchase price of any system that is sold by its vendor.

Item	Year 0	Year 1	Year 2	Year 3	Year 4	Year 5	Year 6	Year 7	Total
Consulting									
Design/engineering									
Operating equipment									
Inventory									
Site preparation									
Cable									
Shipping									
Installation									
Initial training									
Operating supplies									
Insurance									
Equipment maintenance									
Network charges									
Facilities operations									
Training new employees									
Administration									
Cost of capital									
Removal charges									
Salvage value	( )	( )	( )	( )	( )	( )	( )	( )	( )
Total									

Figure 2.   Cost matrix for telephone procurement.

2. Costs of planned system expansion, or savings from planned system reduction, can be listed for the year(s) in which they are planned.
3. Anticipated price changes for maintenance agreements, lease payments, and so on can be expressed as dollar costs at the appropriate points on the matrix.
4. The dollar cost of vendor-provided financing can be shown as "cost of capital."
5. Total cost by year will enable you to analyze cash flow.

Vendor responses should be used to evaluate the total cost during the selection phase. The discussion of that phase will include alternative evaluation methods, such as net present value, payback period, and internal rate of return. The data gathered here will allow use of all these evaluation techniques.

Vendor qualification specifications   There are two categories of vendor qualifications: general capability and specific support capability. These specifications should appear in the RFP in the form of information requirements from each vendor.

General vendor capability can be demonstrated in several ways. The following are examples of information you should consider asking vendors to provide:

1. Names of customers who are using the proposed system
2. Financial rating (Dun and Bradstreet or Standard and Poor's)
3. Annual financial report
4. Financial references (banks or creditors)
5. Profile (size, location(s), age)
6. Local office (functions, size, years in the community, location).

Specific support capabilities relate to engineering, maintenance, training, inventory, and other support services you may require from the vendor. The following are typical details you may request:

1. Support personnel (type, number, location, qualifications)
2. Hours of operation and response time
3. Warranties and/or guarantees.

You should request only information that is pertinent to selection. It is easy to be overwhelmed by irrelevant references, qualifications that do not relate to the system, and other trivia.

General rules and specifications   Policies and requirements that regulate the bid process are the "boilerplate" of the RFP. Several of them, however, require thought and planning:

1. Specific performance assurance (bonds, penalties, payment reserves, progress payments)
2. Accident, liability, and property damage insurance
3. Type of contract (fixed-price, actual cost, or cost "not to exceed"), including limits on excess costs
4. Price versus product (if you state a cost limit, you should let the vendors compete on product; if you require specific product capability, you should let the vendors compete on price; if you try to specify both price and product you may limit competition)
5. Criteria for disqualification (late proposal, nonresponsive proposal, proscribed behavior during procurement process)
6. Installation rules (conformance to building code, uninterrupted service, limits on interference with normal access to facilities, schedule for installation, appearance of the work site)
7. Evaluation criteria and procedures.

The other general rules and specifications should include standard information on proposal deadline, details of any bidders' conference, project coordinator's name, title, and phone number, a schedule of selection process steps and dates, any restrictions on vendor contact with your organization, and guidelines for the format and content of proposals.

Solicitation of proposals
The solicitation phase begins with preparation of the RFP and ends with the receipt of proposals from bidders.

Prepare the RFP   The RFP should contain the four sets of specifications from the planning phase: functional and technical specifications, cost analysis specifications, vendor qualification specifications, and general rules and specifications.

The final draft of the RFP should be reviewed and approved by the entire procurement team.

Issue the RFP   As with other competitive procurements, the RFP should be widely disseminated and, if appropriate, advertised. The RFP should *not* specify "purchase option only" or "lease option only," as these unnecessarily restrict the list of eligible vendors. Your primary concerns should be product, service, and cost. Financing arrangements should be considered only to the extent that they affect cash flow or total cost.

Conduct bidders' conference   The procurement team

should conduct the bidders' conference. Bidders' questions and the team's answers should be recorded and distributed to any bidder who does not attend the conference.

Maintain contact with vendors during proposal preparation It is appropriate and desirable to remain in contact with vendors during their research and preparation of proposals. As a rule, vendors who conduct on-site research produce better, more responsive, and more creative proposals. You should, however, give all vendors equal opportunity and equal restrictions. The procurement team coordinator should regulate and schedule vendor contacts to ensure equal, impartial treatment. (Note: equality of access does not require equality of use. Some vendors may not choose to use all the opportunities you offer.)

Receive proposals Vendors must submit their proposals by the announced deadline. Late proposals should be discarded as the first step in selection.

Selection
The selection phase should be conducted as a series of screenings. Any proposal that fails to pass a particular screening should be eliminated from further consideration. This approach will prevent you from conducting complete evaluations of proposals that do not meet minimum requirements. Proposals that survive each screening may be rated by grades, rank order, scores, or weighted scores. Records should be maintained on all proposal screenings in case of appeals or challenges to the final selection.

General screening Any proposal that is late, or that omits required elements (i.e., vendor qualifications, system description, etc.) should be eliminated from further evaluation.

Functional/technical screening Each vendor's proposed system should be compared to your stated functional and technical specifications. Proposals offering alternatives that are fully described and justified should be evaluated to determine whether or not they are acceptable. Proposals offering "extra" features or capacity should be flagged for special review during cost analysis.

    Functional and technical screening precedes the evaluation of vendor qualifications and cost for the obvious reason that you can't use a technically inadequate system, regardless of cost or vendor qualifications.

Vendor qualification screening Vendors' qualifications should be reviewed before you analyze costs. Low-cost proposals are worthless if the vendor cannot meet deadlines, keep the system operating, and honor the bid price. You should contact all the references of each vendor who is still in the running. First, this may eliminate systems that conform on paper to your functional/technical specifications but do not perform in operating environments. Second, you may identify systems for which the actual installed cost is consistently higher than the bid price.

You should also verify and evaluate the other aspects of vendor qualifications (financial strength, support capability, etc.). You should eliminate proposals from vendors who do not meet your standards. This screening precedes the analysis of cost in order to screen out "low-ball" bids. It will also eliminate disreputable or weak vendors who use low cost as a substitute for service and support. In the increasingly competitive telephone industry you should expect both reasonable cost and satisfactory service.

Cost analysis screening Each remaining proposal should be subjected to a three-part cost analysis: direct cash cost, total cash cost, and total investment cost. First, however, you should validate the accuracy of the useful life, salvage value, inventory cost, inflation factors, and other variables the vendors submit. Unintentional errors and honest disagreements with your stated standards must be resolved and adjusted to ensure that each vendor's costs will represent the actual cost to you of their system.

Direct cash cost The total of all payments to be made to the vendor is the direct cash cost. This is the amount that would appear in a contract with that vendor. Direct cash costs are not valid figures for comparing vendors because of variations in the costs of things you must provide. For example, one vendor's direct cash cost may include property damage insurance on equipment, while another vendor may require you to obtain your own insurance. Such variations must be analyzed in order to identify the *total* cash cost to you of each system.

Total cash cost The total of all payments to be made by you for system-related expenses (whether to the vendor or to some other party) is the total cash cost. The total cash cost of a system is the sum of the system's direct cash cost plus:

1. Cost specification items that the vendor does not provide. Common examples include insurance, network charges, administration, facilities operations, and cost of capital.

2. Personnel employed by you to operate or maintain the
    system. This should be calculated separately for each pro-
    posal because of variations in the labor-intensiveness of
    systems, as well as variations in vendors' offers to provide
    such personnel.
3. Tax revenue from your present system (i.e., franchise and/
    or property tax) that would be lost if you selected a differ-
    ent vendor. Most local governments collect franchise fees
    or utility taxes from the regulated telephone company.
    This revenue will decrease if you buy a telephone system
    from a vendor who is exempt from such charges. Con-
    versely, tax revenue that you would collect from an alter-
    nate system should be subtracted from the total cost of
    that system.

By definition, the vendor is not charging you for these
things, so you must take them into consideration for each
proposal. Total cash costs can then be compared among systems
to identify the least expensive one. The best investment, however, may not have the lowest total cash cost.

Total investment cost   "Opportunity cost" is the cost of using
your limited resources to purchase one item or service instead of
another. Naturally, your organization *must* have a telephone
system, so it is meaningless for you to compare telephone costs
to other opportunities such as roads, police cars, or fire equipment. However, if one proposed telephone system costs less than
another proposed system, the "savings" represent "opportunities" to fill potholes, arrest criminals, or extinguish fires.

When you compute the cost of competitive telephone proposals for total *cash* cost analysis you will invariably identify cost
differences that *appear* to represent real savings, and therefore
opportunities. Cash costs, however, do not take inflation into
account. As we know from recent experience, payments in future
inflated dollars are "cheaper" than payments in current dollars.
Total *investment* cost analysis takes this fact into account and
helps you analyze proposals more accurately by "discounting"
future payments for a telephone system to establish their value
in today's dollars. This may reveal significant opportunity cost
differences between proposals that call for cash in advance and
others that offer deferred payments in the form of financing or
operating leases.

For example, consider two proposals for a telephone system
that has a useful life of five years. Proposal A asks for a cash
payment of $750,000 for equipment and five annual payments of
$50,000 for operating costs—a total cash cost of $1,000,000.

Proposal B asks for five annual payments of $195,000 for equipment (which includes $750,000 for equipment plus 10% interest for financing) and five annual payments of $50,000 for operating costs, for a total cash cost of $1,225,000. When the two proposals are compared, Proposal A appears to provide you with $225,000 in opportunity money.

Investment cash analysis, however, produces a different result. First, you select a discount rate that represents the "value" of your alternative "opportunities." If you have difficulty establishing the value of your opportunities, you could use the rate of interest for short-term Treasury bills. There is no question about the safety of such an investment, so it is a reasonable opportunity discount rate. You may also increase the discount rate by as much as 6 percent to 12 percent to account for risk, such as sudden obsolescence, availability of parts and maintenance, or vendor stability. For the purpose of our example, assume an annual discount of 16 percent. A table of discount rate factors will tell you the rate to be used in each of the future years (the further in the future, the cheaper the dollars, thus the greater the discount).

Figure 3 shows each proposal's cash flow and the discounted present value of each year's cash cost. The total of annual

Proposal A investment cost

Year	Cash cost	×	Discount	=	Present value
0	$750,000		1.000		$750,000
1	50,000		0.862		43,100
2	50,000		0.743		37,150
3	50,000		0.641		32,050
4	50,000		0.552		27,600
5	50,000		0.476		23,800
Total investment cost					$913,700

Proposal B investment cost

Year	Cash cost	×	Discount	=	Present value
0	$ —		1.000		$ —
1	245,000		0.862		211,190
2	245,000		0.743		182,035
3	245,000		0.641		157,045
4	245,000		0.552		135,240
5	245,000		0.476		116,620
Total investment cost					$802,130

Figure 3.   Investment cost analysis of two proposals.

present values is the total *investment* cost of that proposal. The total investment cost of Proposal B is $111,570 *less* than Proposal A. That savings represents your opportunity if you select B, or your cost if you select A.

The procedures described above can also be used to develop three "standard" analyses of investment cost: net present value, internal rate of return, and payback period. Net present value reports the net cumulative savings of one proposal compared to another. Internal rate of return expresses the savings as an interest rate, similar to interest you could earn on idle funds. Payback period tells you the number of years it will take for a system to "pay for itself."

In conclusion, you should evaluate the costs of telephone proposals in three steps: (1) direct cash cost will identify contract payments to vendors; (2) total cash cost will identify the total out-of-pocket expense to you of each system; and (3) total investment cost (net present value, internal rate of return, and payback) will identify your best investment.

You may need to compute additional cost analyses for proposals that offer extra features or capacity. If you determine that you will incur financing costs for the purchase of a system, the cost of capital (interest) must be added to the total cash cost, and the total investment cost must be recomputed. The final task in cost analysis screening is to arrange proposals in order of their total investment cost. You should either select the system that represents the best investment or invite vendors with similar investment costs to make final presentations prior to your selection.

Vendor presentations   The screenings described above may produce a clear "winner," or they may only narrow the field. In the latter case each finalist should be invited to make a presentation to the procurement team. The primary purpose of a presentation is to permit the team to clarify any ambiguity and to pose direct questions to the competitors. The procurement team should meet before the presentations to discuss the questions they wish to ask each finalist. Each presentation session should begin with a short overview from the vendor and then proceed immediately to the question-and-answer phase.

Selection   The conclusion of the process involves selection of a vendor and notification of all bidders of the final decision. The selection initiates your usual process for contract negotiation and approval. You may be asked to explain your decision to unsuccessful vendors, and you may receive appeals. You should establish procedures for these eventualities and include them in the original RFP.

Conclusion

Telephone system vendors offer local governments a three-ring circus of high-technology solutions to communications problems. The products, however, are not priced like sideshow games at three chances for a dollar. In fact, the cost of one spin of the wheel can be hundreds of thousands, or even millions, of dollars. In the high stakes "game" of telephones you can take a chance, or you can manage a choice.

A managed telephone procurement can increase service, control costs, and improve productivity. An unmanaged procurement can leave you with poor service, cost overruns, and unkept promises. The difference between the two is careful planning, competitive solicitation, and dispassionate selection. The result is choice rather than chance.

1. See *Telecommunications Procurement Using Functional Specifications* (Washington, D.C.: National Telecommunications and Information Administration, January 1980).

PART 5

Satellite and Other Advanced Technologies

Beware the Killer Birds

Jonathan Miller

Remember (it seems like ages ago) when the cable business did little more than retransmit programs into obscure Pennsylvania valleys, and when urban cable systems struggled to persuade prospective subscribers that they should pay for the privilege of watching shows that most could already receive via rabbit ears? It was only in the mid-seventies, with the advent of domestic satellites, and their adoption by Home Box Office and Ted Turner, that cable found itself with something really new to sell, and began to transform itself from an anemic fellow traveler of the TV business to the dynamic industry that it has since become.

It would seem from outward appearances that all is well in cableland, and the good times will roll on forever.

But just as conventional broadcasters found themselves taken by surprise at the new vitality of cable in the seventies, the cable people may be finding they are facing a challenger of their own. The reason is "DBS"—direct-to-home broadcasting satellites—that promise to deliver many of the goodies of cable, but without cable systems.

The DBS people look at cities like Chicago and drool at the prospect of putting their micro-dishes on the roofs of the hundreds of apartment blocks that march up unwired Sheridan Road, with master antenna TV hookups to the tens of thousands of apartments below. They look at the exurbia to which so many Americans have gravitated in the last decade, and predict a dish on every roof.

Reprinted from *Cable Business* magazine, published by Television Digest, Inc., 1836 Jefferson Place, N.W., Washington, D.C. 20036.

And they look at people who are now cable customers, and believe that in many cases *they will take these customers away.*

Cable's official spokesmen scoff at the suggestion that DBS will put them out of business. And, in reality, not even the most ardent DBS advocates believe that this will be the outcome. But in the coming DBS wars, some cable systems will be more vulnerable than others, and there could indeed be casualties. Both cable and satellite people agree that if the cable people don't finish wiring up America pretty soon, they're going to find tough competition waiting for them.

Today, a little less than 30% of American homes actually have cable. And even at the current rate of growth, there are likely to be 40 or 50 million homes still without cable when the first U.S. DBS bird roars into orbit, probably some time in late 1985. Between 1986 and 1990, there could be as many as a dozen more DBS birds lofted to orbit, each offering from 3-10 channels of premium and basic programming.

What makes the satellite crowd so gleeful is that with the exception of 2-way services, there will be little that cable can offer that satellites can't offer as well.

So the question naturally arises: Who can do it cheaper?

And the answer, at least at this stage of the game, is that the satellite folk seem to have some economically interesting numbers—especially insofar as delivery of pay-TV is concerned. According to the FCC filings of the DBS contenders, it will cost about $150 million to build and launch each 3-channel DBS bird—around $50 million per actual channel. Since DBS birds won't feature nationwide coverage but will focus their beams on time zones, and because the DBSers want to give consumers the easiest (i.e. the steepest) "look angles" for their dishes, 3 different satellites will be needed to serve the entire contiguous United States. This means the capital cost of the 3 actual channels necessary to cover the entire country runs in the neighborhood of $150 million.

If this can be amortized over 7 or 8 years and 10 million homes, the rough figures work out to it costing a paltry $2 per home per year per channel. Put another way, the distribution cost (for the satellite operator) for a single pay-TV channel looks minimal in comparison with the cost of distributing the same channel nationwide via cable.

For illustration of the economics of distributing pay TV via cable, take the case of Home Box Office. An HBO subscriber pays approximately $10 per month, of which HBO gets about half and the cable operator the rest. Over 12 months, then, it "costs" HBO about $60 per home for the cable gateway for its single channel.

Obviously, the satellite operators will be charging the programmers a lot more than $2 per home per year. This figure would only cover the capital cost of the satellites and the launch. But if one triples this figure to cover the cost of money and the operating costs of the system, and triples it again to cover the satellite operator's mark-up, the price per year to the programmer is still only $18 per home. With the wildest possible estimate of inflation (triple it all again) the figure still is only $54—significantly less than the cost of distributing the same signal via cable. (How much less? If the satellite industry can gain only a $6-per-home-per-year cost advantage, it will have an advantage of $60 million per year on a universe of 10 million homes.)

The reasons for the DBS advantage are numerous. Cost benefits of direct satellite transmission include: (1) no need to win a franchise from cash-strapped local officials, with their understandable tendency to look on a local cable system as a cash cow; (2) no need to supply terminals (since customers will be able to buy the gear themselves for a few hundred dollars); (3) no need to make deals with and pay off the local utilities for poles; (4) no need for maintenance crews to keep the strand operating after thunderstorms; and (5) no need to pay the overheads of thousands of local cable operators struggling to pay off huge bank loans.

Ask the cablemen about these figures and you encounter gentle skepticism. The official line at the National Cable TV Association is that DBS will be complementary to cable, rather than truly competitive. NCTA spokesmen argue that where cable already exists, the satellite people will have a hard time persuading viewers to invest in the antenna and electronics to receive DBS. Further, they say, satellites inherently lack the 2-way capabilities of cable. DBS operators, they add, won't be able to offer home security systems, electronic banking, electronic shopping and the like.

Reese Schonfeld, president of Cable News Network, observing the satellite-cable equation recently, came to an interesting conclusion. Cable, he said, is too valuable to be used for mere distribution of entertainment programs—a task that can be accomplished best by DBS. Cable is for selling, he suggested—predicting that retailers will lease almost all available channels for electronic department stores.

A perhaps more objective view, from a major U.S. telecommunications executive involved in both cable and DBS planning, holds that where cable can't be provided to homes for less than $500 per home, satellites will prevail. Elsewhere, cable will be dominant.

But the fate of the cable industry in an era of DBS probably is mostly in the hands of the cable industry itself. The frequency spectrum, in the final analysis, is a finite resource. Nobody knows how many channels of DBS will eventually be possible—but it's clear that however many can be beamed to earth from DBS birds, innovative cable operators will be able to raise the bet. If there are 40 channels of DBS, cable operators had better be prepared to offer more—and at a competitive price. If DBS offers much of the basic and premium programming available on cable, then the cable industry will have to offer more than programs—expanding its offerings to the variety of information and transactional services (possibly including telephone-type services) that provide much of the grist for the communications futurists.

Don't write the obituaries on cable just yet. Put away the shovels and stop digging the grave. The forward-thinking and effective cable operator, providing more than just entertainment, won't be dislodged by a satellite. Such cable systems will become so entrenched that a thousand and one satellites will fail to knock him off. On the other hand, for the cable operators with obsolete, limited channel, one-way cable systems, the satellites really may prove killers.

The 'Un' Wired Nation? MDS Makes Its Case

Don Franco

In February 1982, Microband Corp. proposed to the FCC an "urban over-the-air wireless cable network" through the construction of five-channel MDS operations offering a wide range of programming. Many cable observers have speculated about the potential threat multichannel MDS could have on cable systems located in the same community. In the following article, firm president, Don Franco, responds to TVC's invitation to explain the Urbanet concept.

"This is a blockbuster proposal," said FCC Commissioner James Quello. "It is one of the most interesting ideas we have seen in a while."

What Commissioner Quello was referring to is the proposal put forth by Microband Corp. for the creation of nationwide "wireless cable" networks, an unwired nation.

Microband would accomplish this by expanding the channel capacity of existing and future MDS stations in the top 50 markets in order to permit MDS-delivered pay TV to compete on equal footing with traditional coaxial cable systems.

Most significant about Microband's proposal is the firm's opinion that it can be accomplished rapidly and inexpensively. In two years or less and at a cost of no more than $35 million, Microband says almost all homes in the top 50 markets could be passed with three multichannel wireless cable systems. In most instances this would be well before coaxial cable could get there.

Today there are MDS stations licensed in approximately 150 markets throughout the United States. Approximately

Reprinted with permission from *TVC* magazine, May 1, 1982.

750,000 subscribers receive programming directly or indirectly via MDS—some seven percent of the pay universe.

MDS' growth can be traced to the development—during the past three years—of low cost reception equipment. This equipment permits individual homes to be wired for as little as $100. Prior to this development, MDS was restricted by its economics to serving only large multi-dwelling units and hotels. Multiple channels will make MDS more efficient.

Multichannel MDS systems will be able to provide urban consumers with premium television and other broadband and narrowband entertainment and information services. Although a substantial demand for these services exists, most urban residents have been unable to obtain them because coaxial cable operators, the primary providers of these services, have been slow to wire the nation's major markets. This situation will not soon change. By the end of this decade, notwithstanding the accelerated pace of urban cable franchising and construction, there will remain substantial uncabled urban pockets and tens of millions of uncabled urban consumers. One forecaster puts the number at 30 million homes not passed by cable, with another 28 million homes passed but not served.

Moreover, Microband believes the economics associated with installation of coaxial cable will preclude a fully wired nation. Capital, labor and regulatory requirements will be particularly inhibiting. These same economics have been instrumental in transforming the cable industry from one made up of a large number of small local companies to one becoming dominated by fewer large, often vertically and horizontally integrated firms with substantial power over both the conduit and the content of the information transmitted.

After an extensive examination of market demand at both the national and local levels and a comparative analysis of the economics of coaxial cable and multichannel MDS, Microband concluded that multichannel MDS can help satisfy the existing substantial market demand for pay TV.

In response to Microband's proposal, NCTA's Tom Wheeler said, "We consider MDS a competing technology. Competition is the name of the game." This is exactly the point. As Microband demonstrated to the Commission, competition will benefit both the public and cable.

Competition sought

Clearly, a fully competitive marketplace—one which will ensure downward pressure on the price of service to the public—is a desirable goal. But this situation does not exist today. There is no competition for each cable subscriber. Overbuilds are few and far between—and where they have been tried they have failed.

By expanding the capacity of all presently authorized MDS stations located in the top 50 markets from one channel to five and by expanding the number of MDS carriers authorized in each of these markets from two to three, MDS will be able to provide the desired competition. But this is not, insofar as cable is concerned, competition to be feared. Rather, it is competition which will improve return on investment for the cable operator.

This is so because franchising authorities force the cable operator to build in all sections of the franchise area. Local officials, responding to pressure from their constituencies, are concerned more about providing universal service than about the cost or efficiency of that service. For example, Warner Amex' franchise proposal for Brooklyn included both profitable and unprofitable areas. This proposal held Warner's overall return on equity to a low 11.3 percent. On the other hand, if only economically viable sections were built, Warner Amex' return would be almost double.

Stated another way, if cable operators were not required to subsidize one part of the market with the fees charged in another part, they would be in a position to lower their price to the public. Assuming that these other areas would have MDS-delivered programming available, the concerns of the city fathers would be satisfied, and cable service would develop at a price far lower than would be possible if the entire area were cabled.

Achieving an effective counter-balance to cable's monopoly status through marketplace factors would also eliminate the necessity for increased Commission and local regulation of cable. As Tom Wheeler said, "That [Microband's proposal for regulation by marketplace forces] is all the more reason for cable to be deregulated at the local level." Microband supports this point of view. But to achieve regulation by marketplace forces requires viable, alternative delivery systems which have sufficient channel capacity to serve the needs of a consumer market ravenous for multiple viewing options.

It has become increasingly evident that, in the long run, single channel systems will not be able to meet marketplace demand. A significant aspect of this general demand for pay TV is that it is now for multichannel or "tiers" of service. A recent Gallup Poll showed that over one-half of the households in the United States desire more than one channel of pay television. With multichannel capacity and telephone-based return circuits, MDS will attain parity with coaxial cable systems.

Speedy pace

Because new technology is not involved—merely the expansion of existing MDS transmission facilities and their use in conjunction with in-place telephone-based data communications facilities—and because MDS facilities can be expanded much more rapidly than cable can be installed, construction in all of the top 50 markets could be completed within 24 months of the first grant, and in some cases, six months after FCC approval.

But even so, MDS will not replace cable. Rather, the technologies will exist side by side. An optimistic projection of multichannel MDS shows that by 1990 the service will be serving only 6 million homes out of some 100 million TV households. If by virtue of its presence, MDS will have fostered lower prices in the marketplace, greater diversity of programs, a separation between content and conduit and increased cable profitability, the wired nation will have been in the public interest.

Rewiring America

_____ Morris Edwards

Communications is converging with other information technologies, and I would like to suggest some ways that government and industry can help us get the most from this most valuable resource.

To understand the importance of communications, it's helpful to draw an analogy with the development of canals, highways and railroads in Britain in the early 1800s. It was these improved distribution channels that gave the Industrial Revolution its tremendous head of steam and powered Britain to economic dominance in the 19th century. Approaching the end of the 20th century, we are moving into the Post-Industrial, or Information Age. And, once again, it will be the distribution channels—in this case communications networks—that will pace the growth of the new culture and the economic power that goes with it.

Unfortunately, our existing communications facilities have tended to hinder the flow of information rather than expedite it. However, thanks to developments with satellites, fiber optics and, most especially, with semiconductor technology, this situation is about to change in a rapid and fundamental way.

Wideband links, digital electronics, interface standards and the information utility

When we consider the types of communications facilities that will be needed for the Information Age to flourish, four requirements emerge. First, there is the obvious need for wideband, or high-speed links to carry the increased amount of information.

Reprinted with permission from _Government Data Systems,_ July/August 1981.

Also, we need digital links in place of the analog facilities designed to handle the voice traffic of the telephone network. The economics, power and reliability of today's semiconductor devices alone mandate this; but there are many other technical reasons for going digital. So much so that, in the future, speech will be digitized and distributed in the same form as computer data.

A third requirement is for some means of allowing different kinds of terminals to talk with each other. If standards existed for these terminals, there would be no problem communicating between them. But, until that happens, the communications network will have to provide a translation service through built-in "intelligence."

In this respect, the ideal communications service has been likened to an electric utility. With an electrical outlet, you can plug in a toaster, light or dishwasher and draw power. Similarly, with an "information utility," you will be able to "plug in" any type of device—be it computer terminal, telephone or facsimile machine—and not only receive information but also feed it into the network for distribution to other designated devices.

Another important parallel with the electric utility is the concept of paying for usage only. This is one of the most revolutionary aspects of the information utility. As soon as you eliminate distance as the criterion for communications charges, and base the pricing on usage instead, you open up a whole new world of applications that were uneconomic before.

Ethernet

This concept of an information utility may seem like a pipedream, but, technologically at least, it is tantalizingly real. Xerox Corp. has already adopted the idea of an information utility in its advertisements for Ethernet, calling it the "Information Outlet." Ethernet is a cable that runs through a building or office complex, interconnecting the various business machines so they can communicate freely with each other. Ethernet has many of the characteristics of an information utility. It operates digitally and at high speed—about 1,000 times faster than a telephone line. Also, it permits communications between devices that do not speak the same language, including non-Xerox computers and terminals.

But Ethernet is only part of the solution. For one thing, you cannot connect telephones to it yet. Also, its range is limited to intra-facility use. Besides Ethernet-type networks, we also need facilities for communications within cities, and for long-distance, inter-city transmissions.

Also, if Ethernet is part of the solution, it is also part of the problem in the sense that it is one of several non-compatible ways to wire an office using a cable. The interface standards groups are looking into this problem, but thus far have shirked their responsibility by adopting two different standards, which is equivalent to having no standard at all.

Integrated business exchange

Another way to wire the office is through a digital private branch exchange (PBX), which is the modern-day version of the old telephone switchboard. As the name implies, these PBXs operate digitally and at reasonably high speeds. Also, unlike Ethernet, they link the telephone into the network along with the business machines. An example of these advanced PBXs is the one introduced last year by an Exxon Company called InteCom. The so-called Integrated Business Exchange (IBX) digitizes speech at the telephone handset and integrates it with data from a business machine so they can both operate at the same time over the same line. Also, the IBX has enough intelligence to allow incompatible terminals to talk with each other.

Satellites

So, all in all, substantial progress is being made in rewiring the office in readiness for the Information Age. What about long-distance communications? Here, the major action centers on fiber optics, and, to a greater extent, on satellites, which can simultaneously interconnect any number of earth stations around the country with high-speed, digital communications channels. Satellites usher in communications charges based on usage, since mileage-based pricing makes no sense when the distances on earth are so small compared to the 45,000-mile round trip to the satellite and back.

Two recent events have given a boost to satellites: one was the success of the space shuttle, which promises not only to reduce the cost of launching satellites, but to make practical the launching of larger satellites with more complex gear aboard to permit even more innovative services; the second was the approval by the Federal Communications Commission for the launching of an additional 20 communications satellites by eight firms, more than tripling the current service capacity.

One firm that has done a great deal to educate the business community about the innovative services possible through satellites is Satellite Business Systems (SBS), which is a partnership of IBM, Aetna Life and Casualty and Comsat General. SBS recently inaugurated its innovative service after a five-year development effort. Through its satellite channels, SBS essentially provides users with a large pipeline to transport all kinds of information between their various facilities. Since compatibility must be provided by the devices at each end, the service is geared to intra-organizational communications, where a network manager can establish the required standards.

Another approach is to include computers and storage devices in the satellite network to provide the translations and conversions required for incompatible devices to talk with each other. This so-called public network service is effective for both intra- and inter-organizational communications, since it can accommodate a number of different terminal types. Both approaches can provide high-speed service, with digitized speech and data integrated over the same links.

One of the key elements of the SBS service is to place the earth stations at the customer's premises, either on the rooftop or in the parking lot. The idea is to eliminate the local telephone loops, which limit both the speed and performance of the end-to-end communications link. However, since it's impractical to place an earth station on every building, the local loop problem can only be solved through a new type of intra-city communications facility.

Even here, though, progress is being made with a new type of digital microwave system. This system uses a portion of the frequency spectrum recently reallocated for this specific application by the FCC. The scheme was first proposed by Xerox as part of a plan to integrate its Ethernet installation to a long-distance service it will offer starting in 1982. Following the FCC ruling, however, a number of other firms are planning to offer similar intra-city communications service.

In fact, starting in June 1981, SBS joined with Tymnet, a supplier of public network services, and a third firm to check out the digital microwave service in San Francisco and New York City. They are also testing cable TV as a possible alternative to the local distribution system. In addition, the test is checking out the interconnection of the intra-city network with long-distance service, using a satellite link provided by SBS between the two cities. Later, the firms plan to extend the test to include a number of Ethernet installations, clearing the way for high-speed digital communications end-to-end from user to user nationwide.

Adopt network standards now
So it's clear that we are making headway on every communications front—intra-facility, intra-city and inter-city. However, progress would be faster with a little encouragement from government and cooperation from industry.

By government encouragement, I mean the setting of legis-

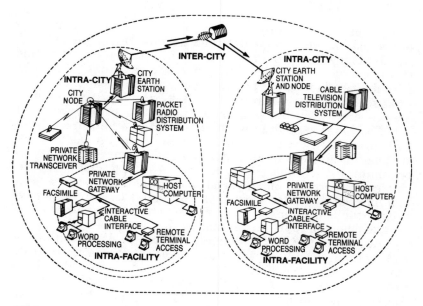

Tests now underway in San Francisco and New York City could lead to intra-city and intra-facility networks that interconnect with inter-city satellite service. The result: high-speed digital communications from user to user nationwide.

lation and regulation to encourage the proper environment for communications growth. For instance, it's quite clear that competition has contributed greatly to the communications advances in the past decade. But AT&T is noticeably absent from all the leading-edge developments. In fact, it's quite staggering to think that the communications giant of the most advanced nation in the world does not yet have a public data network service, unlike a number of communications in other countries.

However, while few can question the need for more competition and less regulation in communications, it's not clear what should be the structure of the industry in general and AT&T in particular. This is something that Congress is wrestling with right now as it attempts to bring the Communications Act of 1934 into the Information Age. Besides the Communications Act, though, there are other government actions that could spur the growth of communications. Not the least important is the development of tax policies that would encourage capital formation and stimulate investment, entrepreneurship and technical research.

For its part, industry can help by being more cooperative in setting the standards needed for universal communications among their diverse products. In the past, industry may have had a reasonable argument for its go-slow policy on network standards because communications facilities were poor and there was no master plan to guide their actions. With the availability of improved communications facilities and a blueprint for network standardization, however, industry no longer has any excuse for dragging its feet in this important area.

The blueprint is the work of the International Standards Organization, whose open systems architecture provides a master plan for all the various types of standards needed to permit communications among different types of terminals. The architecture is divided into layers, and standards can be set a layer at a time without affecting the others. Thus far, standards have been established for three of the seven layers, and work is progressing on a fourth-layer standard.

According to NCR Chairman William S. Anderson, if the U.S. computer industry supported these international standards, it would save 25% of its development resources that are currently wasted on duplication and non-standard programs. Anderson also suggests that users could help in the drive for standardization by supporting those vendors who, in turn, support the international standards. Here again government could obviously play a major role, not as policy maker, but as the largest single user of computers and business machines.

But why should government get involved? The answer goes back to the matter of productivity and the economic power that the information utility will generate. SBS President Robert C. Hall has noted that 45% of U.S. productivity gains over the past six years were attributable to technology, with one-third of that gain coming from computers. The next major step will come from improved communications.

Other countries are starting to realize this. Japan, which is well-known for cooperation between government and industry, has made a strong commitment to communications, both as an economic force and a means to increase the "quality of life." France is working closely with its telecommunications industry in a program called Telematique, whose products include electronic directories, home facsimile, videotex service and the use of a "smart card" for electronic funds transfer and "teleshopping." Meanwhile, the British are deregulating communications and have established a Minister for Information Technology.

In the face of this activity, the U.S. needs a comprehensive national communications policy that will enable it to maintain its traditional leadership position as we enter the Information Age. As users, vendors and legislators, we can all help in this effort. And, as a nation, we all stand to benefit.

PART 6

Emerging Issues:
Privacy, Antitrust,
and Interconnection

Privacy and Cable: How Severe the Problem?

Richard M. Neustadt

Midway through George Orwell's *1984*, the hero meets an old man and asks him how "Big Brother" got started. The answer: things began to go wrong when someone invented two-way TV.

In fact, interactive services will pose significant privacy problems in the real year 1984. No one is proposing to put cameras inside TV sets, but these services will collect and transmit vast amounts of personal information. Existing privacy rules are woefully inadequate to protect that data.

It is important to note that cable did not create these problems and has no monopoly on them. Home banking, shopping, and security services that use the telephone network raise identical issues. Nevertheless, cable gets the press coverage, so it is taking the heat.

After several years of talk, legislators are beginning to act on privacy. Most new local ordinances now include privacy provisions. Illinois has passed a law, and Maryland, New York, and other states are holding hearings on bills. And Sen. Goldwater's cable bill has a privacy provision.

Cable industry leaders have promised to protect subscribers' privacy, and note—rightly—that there have been no abuses. They therefore argue that regulation is unnecessary or, at least, premature. However, there is now a prospect that federal, state and local authorities will adopt hundreds of inconsistent privacy rules, often with little understanding of the technology. That is bad for everyone. The time has come, therefore, for the industry to take the lead in defining a sensible, uniform privacy policy.

The fears that inspire these regulations stem from interac-

Reprinted with permission from *TVC* magazine, May 1, 1982.

tive technology—"pay-per-view" channels; videotex; security systems; home shopping and banking; and "electronic mail." These services raise two distinct issues. First, the signals may be intercepted—that is the same kind of problem as wiretapping. Second, most of these services will collect massive, computerized files on subscribers' behavior—raising the same kinds of dangers as misuse of bank or medical records.

In the interception area, cable subscribers using special equipment may be able to pick up signals coming from or intended for other subscribers. A determined eavesdropper—or an enforcement agent—may put a physical tap on a line or may dial into the central computer that transmits messages and keeps records. Thus private investigators may intercept signals; criminals may tap into systems to decide when to stage burglaries; and law enforcement agencies may want to track suspects' financial transactions and electronic mail.

The federal wiretapping law outlaws private interception of wire communications and says the government can wiretap only with a court order, which judges are to grant sparingly. Unfortunately, this law reaches only "aural" interception, so it leaves all the new services, which use digital signals rather than voice, unprotected. Moreover, this law defines "wire communication" as transmission provided by a "common carrier," so cable seems to be excluded. The Constitution, Section 605 of the Communications Act, and state laws may provide some protection, but the loophole in the wiretapping law should be closed. Sen. Goldwater's bill would do so, and that provision deserves strong support.

Information privacy

The second issue involves the computerized files some interactive systems will create, listing the movies subscribers watch, the things they buy, the money they spend, and the times they enter and leave their homes. Theoretically, operators might be tempted to sell this data to direct mailers, pollsters, potential employers, or insurance and credit investigators. Much of it may be useful to law enforcement agencies. And such records may get into the wrong hands—one can imagine disclosure of politicians' private viewing habits, or electronic robbery by manipulating computer records.

For example, in Columbus, Ohio, the proprietor of a movie theater was prosecuted for showing a sexually explicit film which also appeared on cable. He sought to subpoena the cable company's records—he wanted to use the names of those who viewed the film in his defense. The cable company refused to disclose individual names, and the judge gave the theater owner access only to the total number of people who watched the film, but a tremor went through the community.

While privacy for communications has a long tradition in the country, privacy for information is a new and poorly established principle. Most people are surprised to learn that they have no legal rights to all these records—they belong to the recordkeeper. The federal government has privacy laws on bank and credit records, and some states have additional restrictions, but in most cases system operators are legally free to pass out the records on street corners. Of course, cable operators want to keep their subscribers happy, so most will make sure there are no scandals. However, subscribers are entitled to know what information is being collected and how it is handled, and no sensible cable operator wants to face—for example—an FBI request for access to his records without having an established policy to reply on.

In fact, such a policy for personal records is not hard to develop. Most of the conceptual work was done some years ago by a federal Privacy Commission that studied the use and misuse of medical, bank, and insurance records. Its report and subsequent work in the cable area suggest seven principles for handling personal data:

1. Notice: Subscribers should be notified of a system's two-way capabilities and of any records the company intends to keep.
2. Consent: Written subscriber consent should be obtained for collection of any information from two-way systems, except for data recorded to maintain technical operations, monitor for billing, or detect unauthorized users. The consent form should indicate how the records will be used, including whether they will be disclosed—in individual or aggregate form—to third parties. Customers should be able to sign up for any service without having any individually identifiable information disclosed to third parties.
3. Right to See, Copy and Correct: Subscribers should be able to see and copy—at their own expense—any records concerning them. The company should be obligated to correct any errors.
4. Government Access: Records should be made available to government officials only in response to compulsory legal process. In general, the subscriber should be notified and given an opportunity to contest such access. Notice may be omitted if it would jeopardize an investigation, but the operation should insist on a court order in such cases.
5. Retention: Records should be destroyed when they are no longer needed.

6.   Security: The company should be obliged to keep records
     secure.
7.   Liability: The company should be liable for any damages
     resulting from misuse or unauthorized disclosure of
     records.

Except for notice, these duties should rest on the recordkeeper. Thus, if a cable system offers home banking and the
bank keeps the only records of the transactions, then the bank—
not the cable operator—should be responsible.

The philosophy behind these principles is to let people
know what is happening and give them the right to make their
own decision, *without* having the government decide what kinds
of records should be collected or how they should be used.
Therefore, this code does not forbid anything. Laws should not
prejudge technology—especially in this fast-moving field—or
make assumptions about public attitudes. Some people may
want their records disclosed; for example, when the association
of direct mailers offered several years ago to remove any name
from its members' list on request, more people wanted their
names added than deleted.

Most of the cable privacy rules that have been written so far
use most of these principles. Thus, the code Warner Amex
announced [in October 1981] covers almost all these items.
Warner's code is being incorporated into franchise and subscriber contracts on all its systems, and Warner is insisting that
service providers who use its systems adhere to its code.

Many of the new local cable ordinances also include these
principles, but they vary widely on details. For example, some
require specific subscriber consent for each service that involves
signals from the home terminal, while others rely on notice and
presume consent from the subscriber's decision to use the service. The bills that have been introduced in Maryland and New
York also use all seven principles, but they turn a simple set of
rules into 20 pages each of unnecessary and even harmful detail.
For example:

1.   The Maryland bill bars "systemwide electronic sweeps,"
     except to detect unauthorized interception, do billing, and
     maintain technical operation. This language may inadver-
     tently outlaw system-wide polling, like that on Warner's
     Qube systems.
2.   The New York bill requires one written subscriber con-
     sent to install a two-way system, another to collect data
     from it, and a third to disclose the data. All that paper is
     more likely to confuse subscribers than to help them.
3.   The New York bill also mandates a visual or oral privacy

notice at the beginning of each interactive television show. Subscribers will have been told the rules when they first sign up for the service; there is no reason to make everyone sit through a canned announcement for each show.

Apart from the problems with poorly drafted rules, this is one area where too much diversity is a bad thing. Cable operators and other companies soon will be offering interactive services such as home shopping regionally or even nationally. They will face real problems if they have to organize their data on a town-by-town basis and apply different rules to each set of records.

It is time to build a consensus around simple privacy principles that states and cities can adopt, that Congress can consider and that the companies themselves can use. The industry should take the lead in framing this code.

The Twists in Two-Way Cable

David Burnham

Within a hundred minutes after the televised debate between President Reagan and former President Carter, three-quarters of a million Americans flashed their thumbs up–thumbs down verdict to an electronic voting booth set up by the American Telephone and Telegraph Company for the news division of the American Broadcasting Company. It was the world's largest and fastest public-opinion survey.

Though the ABC survey was conceptually and technically flawed, similar polls will almost certainly become a force in America's political and commercial life. Already, politicians, news organizations, and entertainment shows in Columbus, Ohio, are harvesting public feelings about issues ranging from energy to homosexuality—with the help of an experimental electronic system soon to be ubiquitous in the United States.

The ability to collect and tabulate the almost immediate reactions of millions of Americans to a specific event or problem could ultimately reduce today's prevalent cynical alienation. But it could just as easily lead to a serious weakening of many existing institutions in representative government—and to a gradual erosion in the independent judgment and leadership of public officials.

Two-way interactive television presents these starkly contrasting opportunities for good and evil. It is a computer-powered system that lets the subscriber answer, through his television, any multiple choice questions he is asked, or order

Reprinted with permission from *Channels of Communications*, June/July 1981. © Media Commentary Council, Inc. This article will appear in a book entitled *The New Television*, to be released in the spring of 1983.

any goods and services he is offered. The home terminal of this electronic umbilical cord is a small plastic keyboard, about the size of a thick paperback novel, attached to the family set. When responding to a question, the subscriber "touches in" on one of a series of buttons, the central computer swiftly calculates the proportion of the audience preferring the various options, and the answer is displayed on the home screen.

The interactive television subscriber can also wire his home with sophisticated security and health-monitoring devices, and can increase the number of entertainment, news, and educational programs already piped into his living room.

Cautions

Optimistic futurists and executives selling two-way television have eloquently enumerated the ways the system can enrich America's cultural life, improve the responsiveness of government bureaucracies, and even solve the national energy crisis by eliminating the need to drive to the shopping center or town meeting. The perils, however, have largely been ignored. Some problems:

Instant polling   Two-way television's technical ability to take the pulse of the body politic creates an almost irresistible desire to undertake such polls. But if ABC News was willing to ask the nation who won last October's Presidential beauty contest, why won't ABC News or some other organization decide to measure the nation's mood the next time some nation decides to seize a group of American diplomats? And how would such unreflective and necessarily ill-informed opinion influence the actions of the politician then occupying the White House, or the response of the nation holding the hostages?

Personal privacy   With a fully developed two-way system, many significant details about the life of the subscribing family will be funneled through the system's computer. The information collected by such a computer might well include messages sent by electronic mail to a stockbroker or travel agent, various banking transactions, books ordered at the local bookstore or library, hours devoted to pay-per-view programs that might include soft-core pornography, and the comings and goings of security-service subscribers. Though such details are now frequently recorded by separate organizations, the concentration of data in the computer of one privately owned company presents a major snooping hazard.

Collective privacy   Even if laws and procedures provide each subscriber an ironclad guarantee that personal information will never be improperly shared, neighborhood patterns of book reading, television watching, banking, and electronic shopping will give commercial and political marketing experts a powerful new tool to use on the psyches of unsuspecting customers. When the information collected by the two-way system's computer is merged with the Census Bureau's tract-by-tract information, super salesmen will be able to target their ever-more-refined pitches only at the most susceptible consumers.

Information deprivation   The services offered by two-way interactive television are expensive. The rate for the proposed menu in the Dallas system, for example, is now $47 a month. As such systems become more and more essential in the delivery of cultural, educational, and political information, will the service's price further widen the gap that already separates the poor from the rest of society? Behind this issue lies a complex debate about whether two-way television systems should continue to be owned and operated by traditional business organizations or whether they should be regulated.

Blurring   With the enormous increase in the number of channels entering subscribers' homes comes a diversified selection of programs. One experimental show in Columbus is called the "infomercial," a combination of objective documentary and paid commercial. Some consumer experts fear the marriage of the two forms might do nothing more than mislead and confuse. Lurking behind their concern is the broad question of editorial responsibility. Should the owners of two-way cable systems be considered similar to newspaper publishers and granted First Amendment rights and obligations? Or should cable systems be likened to the telephone company and be required to carry any message an individual wants to send?

Regulation   New government agencies are the traditional panacea for serious social problems in America. But where fragile matters like freedom of speech and privacy are at stake, the cure might well end up being more serious than the disease. Curiously, that possibility has not stopped Sweden, France, and several other European countries from establishing strong government agencies to inspect and license the very computerized information bases that need protection. The prospect of a similar fox being asked to guard the chicken-house in the United States may well be the communication boom's ultimate ironic threat. The dimming but nevertheless powerful memories of the Watergate years remind us that government agencies sometimes abuse their powers.

What's to be done? Many knowledgeable experts believe that mechanical or legal safeguards can be developed. "In my own view, privacy is something of a wash," said Harry M. Shooshan III, the former chief counsel of the House Communications Subcommittee. "Of course, there are problems, but there are also ways technology can enhance personal security."

Charles L. Jackson, a partner with Shooshan in their recently established Washington consulting firm, worked on the same House subcommittee as chief engineer. "The technology gives us an opportunity to enhance privacy as well as undercut it," Jackson said during a conversation in the small firm's new office. "As the system is being built, you can choose the ends that will be served. I do not believe that reliance on the technology by itself creates the hazard to privacy. The question is, what are the goals and what are the values of the people who are creating that system?"

Jackson had to acknowledge, however, that privacy is a subtle issue. "Somehow, we want an assurance that someone who is a political dissident—whether it's John Anderson or even Abbie Hoffman—can live his life without fearing his political opponents will someday be handed a detailed report on his private behavior."

Gustave M. Hauser, co-chairman, president, and chief executive of Warner Amex, emphasized the concern he felt about the privacy of QUBE customers. "I am concerned, others are concerned, we should all be concerned," he said. But like many lawyers, he saw the savior in the law, rather than in technology. "If there is an abuse, there will be a regulation. I am delighted to have any regulation that is appropriate. Why don't we see what the public wants before we start regulating the business? Why don't we build the system and then worry about the things we don't like in it? The people who want to regulate in advance are the people who are going to prevent progress."

The seriousness of the privacy threat, and suggested remedies for it, generate much disagreement. But two-way television's instant polling capability evokes a much more unified sense of concern. "There, there lies the potential for a real problem," said Shooshan. "The media too much dominate the political environment today. If a mayor can take a poll over two-way television about any issue he wants, he can significantly erode the powers of an elected city council or the intent of state referendum laws, which require a certain number of signatures before an issue can be put on a ballot for a direct decision by the voters."

"Instant polling is an area of enormous peril," said Sidney W. Dean, chairman of the City Club of New York's ad hoc committee on cable television, and for seven years a member of the city's advisory committee on the same subject. "Instantaneous surveys on public-policy issues are frightening for a number of reasons. First, there is no time for thoughtful consideration of the issue. Second, from my long experience in marketing research, I know that the hand that writes the questions usually begets the answers."

Robert W. Ross is the senior vice president for law and government relations of the National Cable Television Association. "The consequences? All the consequences are positive," was Ross's reply to a question about the ultimate impact of the cable industry on Americans. "Information is like nuclear power. You can harness it for good or you can harness it for evil. It depends upon what kinds of regulatory structures are set up and how the regulations are applied." But he was far less reassuring when our conversation turned to what he ironically called "the era of plebiscitary democracy." This era will have arrived, he said, the day a politician can say "push button three if you agree with me, and seventeen million hit button three and the decision is made to lock up the Nisei."

Ross recounted his experiences as an ensign in Vietnam, where he believes the nearly instantaneous communication links with Washington robbed him and the rest of the officers of the appropriate authority to make decisions. "If the time comes when an elected official has the ability to swiftly determine how his constituents feel about any issue he is dealing with, it is my guess that the individuality and self-confidence of that official will be undermined," he warned. "A congressman is there to represent his constituents, not just to do his own will. On the other hand, it is simultaneously important for politicians to exercise their own judgments about the rightness of something, rather than responding to pressures of the mob or emotions of the moment."

As two-way interactive cable is installed in a significant number of American homes, many of its fundamental perils—Constitutional, economic, and philosophical—become evident. And Ithiel de Sola Pool, a professor at the Massachusetts Institute of Technology, worries that society might overreact to these perils. "No democracy would tolerate the notion that a reporter's notebook be licensed and subject to inspection by those he is writing about," Pool said. "No democracy would tolerate that a political party's campaign plans be treated the same way, nor that our correspondence with our friends abroad should be compulsorily opened up. But that is exactly what many countries are requiring for computer files. What then happens when a reporter keeps his files on his home computer, or when a political party produces its plans on an intelligent word-processor, or when we write our friends by electronic mail?"

Pool noted the laws recently passed by several European countries. He warned darkly that "a Luddite fear of the computer" is intensifying the centuries of struggle for the protection of personal freedom.

At a time when technological changes are placing large and unanticipated pressures on society, choosing the right course is hard business. Consultant Harry Shooshan recalled Lord Devlin's telling comment about the dangers of our difficult and subtle times: "If freedom of the press or freedom of speech perishes, it will not be by sudden death. It will be a long time dying from a debilitating disease caused by a series of erosive measures, each of which, if examined singly, would have a great deal to be said for it."

The Boulder Decision

Howard J. Gan

In a landmark decision which leaves numerous legal and public policy questions unanswered, the U.S. Supreme Court has ruled that municipalities are *not exempt* from federal antitrust laws *unless* they are furthering or implementing a "clearly articulated and affirmatively expressed state policy." The Court held in the *City of Boulder* case[1] (by a 5-3 vote) that in the absence of a clear state policy authorizing the actions taken, local governments are as subject to antitrust suits as are private businesses.

The issue before the Court was whether actions taken by a city, pursuant to its broad "home rule" power, should be entitled to the same type of antitrust exemption granted to the actions of state government. The decision held that policies originated by a city are not entitled to the same deference as policies of the state, and are therefore subject to antitrust scrutiny. The Court addressed only the issue of immunity or exemption from antitrust suits. It did not attempt to determine whether or not Boulder had actually violated the antitrust laws or what remedies (such as treble damages) might be available if a violation were to be found.

Referring to the issue of ultimate liability for antitrust violations, the decision noted that the local government actions might be judged by different antitrust standards than are applied to private businesses, stating at footnote 20, "[i]t may be that certain activities, which might appear anticompetitive when engaged in by private parties, take on a different complexion when adopted by a local government." Thus, although they

Howard J. Gan is General Counsel, Cable Television Information Center, Arlington, Va. This analysis represents the author's opinions and does not purport to offer legal advice or counsel to any individual or entity.

may not be exempt from antitrust scrutiny, municipalities (including all subdivisions of the state) may be judged by different standards than normally applied to the actions of private businesses.

The full meaning and impact of the decision for communities involved in cable television franchising, regulation or renegotiation will remain clouded until various test cases (including the remanded *Boulder* case) wend their way through the courts. While it is evident that state legislation can shield cities from the antitrust attack, it remains unclear what specific legislative language will be held sufficient to meet the Court's test for a finding of immunity.

Cities are most vulnerable in those states which have not expressly authorized local franchising or regulation of cable television. In other states where legislatures have simply granted local governments broad authority to regulate cable, the courts will examine whether existing expressions of state policy are sufficiently explicit in order to exempt municipalities from antitrust litigation. Even where a state agency shares regulatory jurisdiction over cable with local governments, it is by no means certain that local actions will be automatically protected.

It is too early to tell whether this case will precipitate a large number of antitrust suits against cities. However, there is no question that it will have a "chilling effect" on many regulatory decisions, since municipalities without immunity face the prospect of lengthy and expensive legal defenses if their actions are challenged, not only in cable television matters, but in many other areas traditionally regulated by local government. The opening sentence of the dissenting opinion, written by Justice Rehnquist, projects such an impact: "The Court's decision in this case will... impede, if not paralyze, local governments' efforts to enact ordinances and regulations aimed at protecting public health, safety and welfare, for fear of subjecting the local government to liability under the Sherman Act." While we may hope that Justice Rehnquist's view will turn out to be an overstatement of the case, it will probably take several years of litigation before the implications of *Boulder* are clear. In the interim, while municipalities may not have sweeping immunity from antitrust lawsuits, we believe that reasonable governmental actions based upon a clear legislative record are unlikely to result in a finding of either liability or monetary damages.

Background: the antitrust context
In its decision the Court refers to the federal antitrust laws as "the Magna Carta of free enterprise... as important to the preservation of economic freedom as the Bill of Rights is to the protection of our fundamental personal freedoms." Simply

stated, the federal antitrust laws were enacted for the broad purpose of insuring competition in the marketplace. More specifically, these laws were intended to break up business "trusts" which had developed a powerful stranglehold on various commercial enterprises during the mid 1800s. These trusts were able to restrain or totally eliminate their competitors through concerted action. The Sherman Act in particular was aimed at preventing companies from acting in concert to restrain competition or monopolize markets for products or services. Its provisions were clearly intended to apply to the actions of private businesses. However, neither the antitrust laws nor the legislative history of the acts addressed the question of whether states or their subdivisions could be subjected to antitrust liability for actions which arguably restrain trade. Subsequent case law has provided guidance on how these laws are to be applied.

The "Parker Doctrine": antitrust exemption for "state action"

The landmark case of *Parker* v. *Brown*, 317 U.S. 341 (1943), addressed the question of whether the anticompetitive actions of a state government are exempt from the federal antitrust laws. In what came to be known as the "state action" exemption or "Parker doctrine," the Supreme Court held that ". . . nothing in the language of the Sherman Act or its history suggests that its purpose was to restrain a state or its officers or agents from activities directed by its legislature." The Court found that under our dual system of government, the states have sovereign power. This sovereignty is limited only to the extent that the U.S. Congress, constitutionally relying upon the supremacy of federal law, has specifically preempted or subtracted from the states' powers.

Parker held that a state policy to replace or limit competition by imposing state regulation in its place (in this case to prop up raisin prices), was a valid exercise of the state's sovereign powers and not subject to attack under the federal antitrust laws. In effect, the Court found that in the absence of a finding of specific federal intent to preempt state actions, deference should be given to a state's power to determine its own economic policies. The "state action" doctrine remains valid today, although subsequent court decisions have somewhat narrowed its scope.

The *Lafayette* case: a city is not a state

Following the 1943 *Parker* decision it was generally assumed that since local levels of government are merely subdivisions or instrumentalities of the state, they should be entitled to an implied exemption from the antitrust laws. That is, local government action should be viewed as constituting "state action" for purposes of antitrust scrutiny. However, the concept of a sweeping implied antitrust exemption for municipalities was laid to rest in the 1978 *City of Lafayette* case,[2] involving a city-owned power and light company.

In *Lafayette*, the Supreme Court rejected the city's claim that it was automatically exempt from the operation of the antitrust laws under the state action doctrine. A plurality opinion (four justices) held that cities, as subdivisions of states, do *not* have equivalent sovereign powers and "do not receive all federal deference of the states that create them." The Court found the *Parker* doctrine to be limited to antitrust exemptions for official action directed, authorized or contemplated by a state. It suggested that "serious economic dislocation" could result if cities were free to place their own interests above the national economic goals embodied in the antitrust laws.

The Court emphasized that a state could *authorize* municipal activities which otherwise might be attacked as anticompetitive and, thereby, cloak municipalities with the state's sovereign exemption from liability. It indicated that the *Parker* doctrine provides municipalities with antitrust immunity only so long as they are acting "pursuant to state policy to displace competition with regulation or monopoly public service." Such state policy had to be "clearly articulated and affirmatively expressed."

However, *Lafayette* left room for interpretation because Chief Justice Burger's concurring opinion (making a 5-vote majority) relied on a more narrow ground for finding that the city was not exempt. He suggested that because the city, as owner of the local power company, was acting in furtherance of its business or "proprietary" activities, rather than more traditional "governmental" activities, it was not entitled to claim a *governmental* exemption from antitrust scrutiny. Since there was no clear majority opinion in *Lafayette*, it was hoped that future court decisions might reinforce this distinction between "proprietary" and "governmental" actions. However, the *Boulder* decision failed to offer any support for such a distinction, but rather reiterated the plurality's view.

The *Boulder* case

Background   Community Communications Company (CCC), owned by TeleCommunications, Inc., operated a cable system providing service to approximately one-third of the city of Boulder in an area with poor television reception. From 1966 to 1979 CCC provided basic television retransmission services under a 20-year, nonexclusive permit (granted to CCC's predecessor in 1964). In 1979, CCC informed the city of its plans to complete wiring of Boulder and to provide additional programming. During this period another company expressed interest in building a new cable system in the city. The Boulder city council, recognizing that cable TV companies will virtually never "overbuild" a cable system where one already exists, considered adopting a construction moratorium to insure that the remainder of the city would remain unwired while it contemplated what action to take concerning possible competitors. At this point CCC began accelerating construction of its system.

After hearing oral arguments by the interested parties, the city council voted to impose a 90-day moratorium on the expansion of CCC's cable coverage into new areas. The ordinances adopted expressly stated that the purpose of the moratorium was to prevent CCC from wiring the entire community and thereby hindering the ability of other companies to compete in Boulder. The city found both economic and physical reasons to show that CCC's accelerated wiring of the entire city would threaten to foreclose any future competition and further entrench its existing *de facto* monopoly.

CCC filed suit in U.S. district court seeking a preliminary injunction to prohibit the city from enforcing the moratorium, charging that the city was engaged in a conspiracy to restrain trade by preventing CCC from extending its service to new customers. The city claimed that its acts were (1) a valid exercise of its "home rule" power to act in local matters, granted pursuant to the Colorado constitution, and (2) exempt from antitrust scrutiny as "acts of government" authorized by the state, and therefore qualifying for antitrust exemption under the *Parker* "state action" doctrine.

Despite the city's claim that its actions were not only immune from antitrust attack but designed to foster competition and not preclude it, the district court granted a preliminary injunction, stating that the *Parker* exemption was "wholly inapplicable" and that the city was therefore subject to antitrust liability. The district court said:

Most simply stated, Boulder has attempted to restrict the lawful business of [CCC] by preventing it from obtaining new customers for three months while potential competitors submit proposals for serving those same customers. The motivation may be to foster competition in the long run, but the direct and immediate effect is a restraint of trade and an artificial and unreasonable geographical market allocation.

The city appealed the decision, and on May 28, 1980, the court of appeals reversed the lower decision, finding the city's moratorium to be a legitimate exercise of its home rule powers and exempt from antitrust liability under the *Parker* doctrine. The appeals court cited the test formulated by Chief Justice Burger in his concurring opinion in *Lafayette*, finding that the city's actions were "governmental" rather than "proprietary" in nature and within its broad, state-granted constitutional powers of home rule. The court held that the city's regulations represented the only controlling state or local government policy in the matter which therefore satisfied the state action test.

The Supreme Court's decision   The Supreme Court reversed the court of appeals in a majority opinion which closely followed the plurality opinion of the *Lafayette* case. The Court held that city action cannot constitute "state action" in the absence of any clear and affirmative state policy addressing the subject. The decision provided no support for distinguishing between "governmental" and "proprietary" actions for antitrust exemption purposes.

The Court reiterated the following basic points:

1. Our "dual" system of government provides sovereignty to the federal and state governments. Cities are not sovereign and are not entitled to the federal deference given to states under the antitrust laws.
2. The *Parker* "state action" exemption applies to actions or policies of the state government, and may be claimed by cities only if their actions are furthering or implementing a "clearly articulated and affirmatively expressed" state policy.
3. Home rule power may guarantee local autonomy but does not by itself place the city in the position of the state for antitrust exemption purposes. City action on matters in which there is an absence of any state legislation cannot be said either to be "contemplated" by the state or implementing a state policy.
4. Unless the state has affirmatively addressed the subject, the city's action cannot be seen as "comprehended within the powers granted" by the state.
5. With regard to a finding of actual violation of the antitrust laws, certain activities, which might appear anticompetitive when engaged in by private parties, may take on a different complexion when adopted by a local government.

The Court concluded its opinion by stating that the *Boulder* decision "does not threaten the legitimate exercise of governmental power, nor does it preclude municipal government from providing services on a monopoly basis." A state may direct and *authorize its instrumentalities* to act in a way which, if it did not reflect state policy, would be inconsistent with the antitrust laws.

Justice William F. Rehnquist, in his dissenting opinion (joined by Chief Justice Burger and Justice O'Connor), argued that the decision ". . . effectively destroys the 'home rule' movement in this country, through which local governments have obtained, not without persistent state opposition, a limited autonomy over matters of local concern." In addition, he stated that the Court's distinction between the actions of cities and states has "no principled basis" and that municipal ordinances should be no more susceptible to invalidation under the Sherman Act than are state statutes. Furthermore, he suggested that the Court should have and could have accomplished the same result without subjecting local governments to the possibility of being found liable for treble damages.

Examining state statutes: who passes the test?

In the aftermath of *Boulder*, local governments face new uncertainties in their handling of cable television matters. The Court's decision forces municipalities to confront two basic questions:

1. Does there exist a *state* policy which is sufficient under the standard enunciated in the *Boulder* case to exempt municipalities from antitrust liability?
2. If state policy is either questionable in terms of its specificity or nonexistent, what issues should be of concern to local governments and what can they do to minimize the likelihood of antitrust liability?

A survey of state cable legislation, based in part upon publications of the Federal Communications Commission, has shown that:

1. Eleven states provide for cable television regulation administered in whole or part by a state agency.
2. Fifteen other states have conferred some form of cable TV franchising or regulatory authority on local governments.
3. Twenty-four states have not granted specific cable regulatory authority to local governments.

It is apparent that in the 24 states which have not granted cable regulatory authority to local governments, municipal actions are clearly not exempt from antitrust scrutiny. There simply is no expression of state policy, and under the *Boulder* decision neutrality by the state cannot justify a local exemption.

In the 15 states which have granted cable regulatory authority to local governments, only a state-by-state analysis of the specific legislative authority will permit a judgment as to whether existing state policy may be sufficient to warrant a municipal exemption. That question is discussed more fully in the following section.

Of the 11 states in which there is oversight by a state agency, only those which regulate exclusively at the state level and do not permit any local regulation can be totally unconcerned about *Boulder*. In the remaining states which share regulatory authority with local governments, a case-by-case analysis will be necessary.

What constitutes a "clear and affirmative" state policy?

The fundamental difficulty with the *Boulder* decision is that it leaves open for interpretation by lower courts the question of what constitutes a "clearly articulated and affirmatively expressed state policy" sufficient to warrant a municipal antitrust exemption. It remains uncertain how specific and detailed state legislation must be in order to meet the *Boulder* test, although the language of the decision and the precedents cited provide some guidance.

The Court focused much of its attention on both the court of appeals and Supreme Court plurality opinions in the *Lafayette* case, mainly because other "state action" precedents do not deal primarily with city-state relationship. While the opinion stressed that municipal actions must be shown to further or implement state policy in order to be exempt from antitrust scrutiny, it did not clarify whether a legislative policy must *specifically* state an intent to displace competition with regulation or monopoly public service, or whether this intent may be inferred from the statutory language, the legislative history or other factors.

The Supreme Court appears to cite with approval the circuit court's decision in *Lafayette*, which directed the lower court on remand to examine "whether the state legislature *contemplated* [emphasis added] a certain type of anticompetitive restraint." The appeals court described the applicable standard as follows:

[I]t is *not necessary to point to an express statutory mandate for each act* which is alleged to violate antitrust laws. It will suffice if the challenged activity was clearly within the legislative intent. Thus, a trial judge may ascertain, *from the authority given a governmental entity to act in a particular area, that the legislature contemplated the kind of action* complained of. On the other hand, . . . the connection between a legislative grant of power and the subordinate entity's asserted use of that power may be too tenuous to permit the conclusion that the entity's intended scope of activity encompassed such conduct. . . . A district judge's inquiry on this point should be broad enough to *include all evidence which might show the scope of legislative* intent [emphasis added].[3]

Later, in referring to the passage above, the Court suggests that if authority is granted by the state, this ". . . necessarily implies an *affirmative addressing of the subject* by the state" [emphasis added]. But since the state of Colorado had no stated policy whatsoever, the Court found ". . . no interaction of state and local regulation." The Court did not address the question of whether there must be any "active state supervision" of an anticompetitive policy.

All of this leaves the federal district courts in the position of attempting to sort out exactly what legislative language or expression of legislative intent will be required in order to find a municipal exemption.

Using a practical example may be helpful in examining these questions. One of the most basic issues which will arise in the antitrust context is the common practice of granting only one franchise in a given community. Although there may be competition for the franchise itself, a municipality which permits only one of several applicants to provide cable service may be accused of restricting competition. Absent an antitrust exemption, the municipality may be forced to defend and justify its alleged anticompetitive actions in court, since antitrust suits are seldom dismissed prior to discovery and other fact-finding procedures.

In states with shared state and local cable regulatory authority, the existence of "active state supervision" of franchising and regulation by a state agency may lend support to a finding of a municipal exemption. A trial court may be more likely to find a municipal exemption where the legislature has established a statewide cable regulatory scheme, actively supervised by a state agency, even if no explicit expression of a state policy to limit or displace competition exists. The Court did not indicate that active state supervision of municipal actions is necessary so long as a clear state policy can be established.

The language of the Massachusetts state cable statute, for example, does not explicitly express a state policy to restrict competition. However, the statute does state that a municipality shall choose *"that applicant* or those applicants" (emphasis added) it believes "will best serve the public interest." This language may be read to indicate that the state has not only contemplated, but has affirmatively authorized, a municipality to limit competition by selecting a single applicant, if it wishes to do so. And, since there is active supervision in the form of a state

cable commission, it could reasonably be inferred that the state
legislature intended to give municipalities the authority to restrict competition, subject to the state's oversight. If such intent
were found, an exemption could be granted.

Fifteen states authorize municipalities to license and regulate cable TV pursuant to state statutes which are broad in
scope. Typical statutes do not contain any explicit, affirmative
expression of a state policy to limit competition. These statutes
are normally permissive in nature, simply providing for local
authority to issue one or more licenses or franchises and adopt
appropriate regulations. Considering the *Boulder* opinion's emphasis on the need for a clear and affirmatively expressed state
policy, it is uncertain whether such statutes could pass muster
under the Court's test. In these states, there is generally no state
oversight or supervision which, although not necessarily required, could be viewed as evidencing a state policy.

Based on the circuit court's opinion in *Lafayette*, a court
may seek to adduce from all available evidence whether the
legislature "contemplated the kind of action complained of,"
which could be inferred from the legislative history. Since the
Boulder opinion does not attempt to define how explicit state
legislation must be in order to constitute a clear and affirmative
policy, it leaves federal district courts with substantial latitude
in making such a determination. Of course, there is no question
that the more specific the state legislative language and intent,
the more likely a municipal exemption will be found.

If a municipal action is not immune, what then?

If a city is sued on antitrust grounds, and if there is no threshold
finding of municipal immunity, a court will have to determine
whether a violation of the antitrust laws has occurred. Cities
could be subject to antitrust scrutiny under both a "per se"
violation analysis and the "rule of reason." Under a per se
analysis, if it is found that specific types of behavior (such as
price-fixing) have occurred, no real defense can be offered, and a
summary judgment may be issued. It is conceivable that rate
regulation, as one example, could be challenged under a per se
violation analysis. However, there are precedents to indicate
that a per se analysis would not be applied to governmental
activities. Support for this view may also be found in the Court's
statement that "certain activities which might appear anticompetitive when engaged in by private parties, take on a
different complexion when adopted by a local government."
Thus, a per se analysis is highly unlikely to be applied by a court
scrutinizing municipal actions.

The rule of reason is used to determine whether an *unrea-*

sonable restraint of trade has taken place. This requires a case-by-case analysis that examines the actions taken, the relevant market for a service as well as other economic and competitive factors. As the Cable Television Information Center noted in its *Boulder amicus curiae* brief to the Supreme Court, the rule of reason requires each factual situation and regulatory mechanism to be evaluated separately. Under this particularized analysis, granting a single franchise, for example, might be upheld in a particular community context, while a similar scheme might be held invalid in a different factual setting. In addition, although it is unclear how the rule of reason would be applied to a local government, arguably it would require balancing the degree of anticompetitive restrictiveness against the procompetitive effects. This would tend to increase the *ad hoc* nature of decisions. As a result, the validity of municipal regulations will not be subject to any general principles but will require extensive case-by-case litigation.

Justice Rehnquist, in his dissenting opinion, expressed a similar concern that under a rule of reason analysis, courts may engage in essentially standardless inquiries into the reasonableness of local regulations, deciding whether local statutes are reasonably related to the ends for which police power may be validly exercised.

In order to find liability under section 1 of the Sherman Act, however, it must be shown that there has been a conspiracy, combination or contract for the purpose of restraining trade. As will be discussed shortly, it is quite unlikely that legitimate governmental actions will be found to have *violated* the federal antitrust laws so long as they are based on reasonable and supportable legislative determinations.

Federal or state legislation   It would seem that the most obvious course of action for local governments would be to lobby for federal and/or state legislation that contains the "magic language" necessary to provide them with antitrust immunity. However, this may be easier said than done. Other interested parties, including cable companies, AT&T and other industries will be stalking the halls of Congress and state houses lobbying for their own causes. The risk is that cities may get something more (or less) than they have bargained for in pursuing legislation. However, the National League of Cities and state municipal organizations may decide it is a battle worth fighting.

Another factor is that once state legislators begin to address this issue, state public utility commissions or other state agencies may want to obtain jurisdiction over cable—a result neither cities nor the cable industry may find desirable. If PUCs take over, municipalities could lose their local regulatory powers and the cable industry might be well on its way to what it perceives as dreaded utility or common carrier status.

The franchising process   Some cities may seek to halt their franchising process until the issue of liability is resolved. Others may incorporate provisions in ordinances and contracts requiring applicants to defend the municipality in any lawsuit arising from a franchise award. It would be wise to take a cautious approach to franchising and to develop a clear and complete legislative record as to the need or justification for various actions taken. In addition, since a conspiracy between the municipality and the cable company may be alleged as part of an antitrust complaint, local officials should limit off-the-record contacts with representatives of franchise applicants.

As to whether single versus multiple franchises should be granted, we believe that it is generally in the public interest to award a "single, nonexclusive" cable franchise for a given geographic area, although every factual situation must be evaluated separately. (While granting a single nonexclusive franchise may constitute a *de facto* exclusive franchise, the municipality retains the right to grant additional franchises if it wishes to do so.) Economies of scale combined with the attributes of a stable and certain economic marketplace are likely to benefit the community in terms of lower subscriber rates, low-cost or free community communications services for nonprofit groups and higher technology facilities.

Furthermore, integrated and interconnected cable systems serving the entire franchise area may provide educational, police, fire, health and other services, which are important attributes of modern cable systems. Communities may wish to establish standards requiring any applicant to serve all portions of the franchise area (subject to population density limitations). In this way, even if more than one franchise is granted, companies will not be permitted to "cream skim," serving only the more desirable portions of the communities.

Municipalities granting single, nonexclusive franchises may be able to justify such action as a reasonable restraint of trade and a legitimate exercise of local regulatory authority based on a number of considerations. The first is the municipality's traditional police power to protect and promote the public health, safety and welfare. Factors such as having several different companies digging up the streets, installing multiple wires and electronic equipment on poles, as well as other hazardous, disruptive or unsightly practices may be considered legitimate police power concerns. In addition, there are legal and policy precedents to support selective or discretionary municipal licensing and procurement practices which have been based on a fair and competitive application process. Cable systems do have unique attributes which may be cited as additional support for different treatment from that applied to other products or services.

Since granting a single franchise may be one of the acts most likely to precipitate an antitrust suit (by losing applicants), municipalities should carefully review relevant state statutes to determine whether there is legislative support for the proposed actions. Again, all possible legal and public policy justifications should be recorded, including any state legislation, police power-related concerns, economic considerations and public interest benefits in terms of improved services and rates to the community. It may also be wise to document the fact that actions taken were based on informed judgments after consideration of all available alternative courses of action.

Cities with existing cable systems   Communities which currently are served by cable systems could face different antitrust problems from those now going through the franchising process. Cities where franchises are about to expire and those with older twelve-channel systems may find themselves confronted by one or more new applicants seeking to obtain a second franchise. This may be a mixed blessing due to the legal challenges which could arise over the conflicting interests of the existing franchisee, new franchise seekers and the city itself.

It is now becoming more likely than ever that cable companies may seek permission to "overbuild" existing franchises with the hope of eventually taking over the existing company or putting it out of business. There are several reasons for this. In the past there have been both economic disincentives and an unspoken agreement among cable companies not to "claim jump" existing franchises. This attitude may well change due to the *Boulder* decision and new economic pressures.

As long as a large number of cities are without cable service, competition among companies seeking new franchises will be focused on these communities. However, within one or two years, most of the more desirable areas will have awarded franchises, and the available markets will become more limited for those companies pursuing continued growth. Since the cost of acquiring existing systems continues to skyrocket, the economic disincentives to "overbuild" certain markets may become less pronounced. This is particularly true in very highly penetrated markets (70% or higher subscribership). Furthermore, large, multiple-system operators may be willing to undercut the rates of competitors and wait out negative cash flows until they can dominate the market. As a result, municipalities may be faced with deciding whether to grant additional franchises in areas already served by cable.

Communities may be most vulnerable as the time for expiration of the existing franchise approaches. As discussed above, new companies may seek franchises to overbuild or replace the existing system operator. At the same time, the existing company will seek to protect its investment and prevent the city from replacing it with another company. Thus, either the existing operator or new applicants may pose an antitrust threat where (1) the city *negotiates* only with the existing cable company and refuses to consider new applicants or (2) the city seeks to *replace* the existing company with a new company at the end of the franchise term, allowing the existing franchise to expire.

In most instances, companies will not actually file suits against cities, but they may use the mere threat of a suit as a tactical weapon against cable operators and cities.

Although these situations may pose more difficult antitrust problems, municipalities will probably be less vulnerable if they develop a clear record establishing the legal, economic and public-interest justifications for the actions taken. Federal district courts are likely to grant a substantial degree of latitude to local government decisions which are shown to be reasonable and well considered. However, caution is in order because there is a greater likelihood of lawsuits in franchise renegotiation situations. Moreover, the economic and policy factors should be carefully considered because it may be appropriate to replace the existing franchisee or grant additional franchises in some circumstances.

Once again, off-the-record *ex parte* contacts with company representatives should be restricted. No one wants to be named co-conspirator if it can be avoided. Official government actions should be kept official to limit any accusation of collusion with interested parties.

Municipal ownership   More cities than ever before are considering partial or complete municipal ownership. Unless specifically authorized by state statute to preclude other competitors, municipalities which become owners of cable systems may find themselves the target of antitrust suits if they refuse to grant additional franchises to private companies. In addition, companies unwilling to sue or overbuild each other may not have the same compunctions in their dealings with a municipally owned system.

The question of liability may also be more complex in a municipal ownership context. It may not be correct to assume that we are totally rid of the concept of distinguishing between "governmental" and "proprietary" actions. The *Boulder* decision simply stated that in the absence of a clear state policy, governmental actions are not automatically *exempt* from antitrust scrutiny. However, it is quite possible that in a given instance, a court could find that a purely governmental action (i.e., licensing and regulating a private company) should be judged by a different standard of liability than an action in which the municipality has a "proprietary" interest (i.e., government ownership). The question is untested. However, there is reason to believe that a court may more closely scrutinize municipal actions in such a context, since the city has more than a strictly governmental interest at stake. In such cases a court may apply standards of antitrust liability more akin to those it would apply to a private business. Therefore, communities involved in municipally owned systems should be even more cautious in their approach than those which are simply licensing and regulating private companies. As is true of other municipal actions, municipal ownership probably can be successfully defended from attack if a reasonable and proper local legislative record is developed.

Impact on the cable industry: a double-edged sword

While some in the cable industry may perceive *Boulder* as a clear-cut victory, it may turn out to be a double-edged sword. One reason is that the tacit understanding not to overbuild existing franchises may fall by the wayside over time. This could be a highly divisive issue for the cable television industry. Moreover, cable companies will undoubtedly find themselves named co-defendants or co-conspirators in most antitrust suits filed against cities, subjecting them to substantial legal fees and possible liability for treble damages. In addition, communities wishing to avoid possible antitrust litigation may begin more frequently to award duplicative franchises of their own accord, posing new economic problems for existing cable operators. Finally, if state governments become more deeply enmeshed in cable regulation, the industry may be more strictly regulated by state public utility commissions or other state agencies than they are by local governments.

Summary

Despite the uncertainty that remains following the Supreme Court's decision, it is unlikely that the sky is falling or that a tidal wave of antitrust suits will require every city attorney's office to double its staff to avoid treble damages. There is no question that more antitrust suits will be filed, if only as a tactical manuever by some companies either to protect existing franchises or to expand into additional markets. Until a sufficient number of test cases are litigated through the appeals process, we simply will not know how the district courts will interpret the *Boulder* decision for purposes of finding a sufficiently clear and affirmative expression of state policy to justify municipal immunity, or what standards of liability will be applied. However, even if no immunity is found we doubt that legitimate and reasonable municipal actions will be found to violate the antitrust laws or that monetary damages will be assessed even if violations are found.

Obviously, municipal officials will sleep easier if Congress or the state legislatures adopt explicit legislation to shield local governments from lengthy, complex and costly litigation. In the meantime, local officials would be well advised in dealing with cable television franchising or renegotiation to exercise caution and develop clear, complete and legally supportable legislative records for any actions they may take. Off-the-record contacts with company representatives should be limited to avoid the appearance of collusion or conspiracy.

For the time being, municipalities should probably carry on their affairs while doing everything possible to protect themselves from liability under existing state law. In the end, it will be several years before we will know whether the effects of the *Boulder* decision will fulfill the dire predictions of Justice Rehnquist's dissent or be defused by favorable actions in the courts and state legislatures.

1. *Community Communications Co., Inc.*, v. *City of Boulder, Colorado et al.*, 50 U.S.L.W. 4144 (January 13, 1982).
2. *City of Lafayette* v. *Louisiana Power Light Co.*, 435 U.S. 389 (1978).
3. 532F.2d, 434-435 (footnote omitted).

Vital Links: Interconnection of Cable Systems

Linda J. Camp

Cable has experienced tremendous development over the past decade and a high level of excitement and optimism exists about its capability to deliver a variety of new services. Many of these services will be most cost effective and useful on a regional basis, rather than on a single local cable system. However, it is not economically or technically feasible to wire on and on from the headend. Signals can travel only so far through the cable until degradation over distances creates a natural end to the cycle. And since cable is normally franchised on a local basis, more often than not a system is limited to jurisdictional boundaries by the political process as well. Thus, for both technical and political reasons, cable interconnection can be an important consideration.

The term "interconnection" can have several different meanings in discussions of cable television. Broadly defined, interconnection refers to the linking of cable with other communication technologies to increase the capabilities of the system. Interconnection is also used to describe the linking of two or more cable systems, as well as the connection of hubs within an individual system. Most of this article focuses on interconnection of cable systems.

Benefits and applications of system interconnection

Although local orientation is one advantage of a cable communications system, it is also a drawback. The limited reach of a

Reprinted with permission from *The Community Medium,* volume 1 of *CTIC Cablebooks,* edited by Nancy Jesuale with Ralph Lee Smith (Arlington, Va.: Cable Television Information Center, 1982).

single system means that services can be targeted to a clearly identified population—but not all potential recipients of some cable-delivered services will reside in a franchise area. In addition, cable's limited reach means that certain economies of scale enjoyed by other communications technologies are often not possible. By interconnecting systems, these limitations can be overcome so that both public service and commercial applications will be more likely to develop.

Community programming   In the past, cable has been touted as a medium for community programming. Yet in some instances local origination programming has been slow to develop, partially because it is expensive. High-quality origination programming requires sophisticated equipment and facilities that can have an initial price tag of $500,000 or more. Ongoing costs of program production and skilled staff can run into hundreds of thousands of dollars over the life of the franchise, depending on the scope of the effort. This amount is a substantial commitment for any cable operation, but especially for small systems. Likewise, access programming can be expensive. Smaller communities may not have the resources to program a channel full time on an ongoing basis.

Interconnection offers at least one solution to the problems of high cost and underutilization of community channels. Where several systems are reasonably adjacent, it is possible to interconnect the access and local origination channels. Rather than building costly studios in each community, a single local origination facility could be constructed to accommodate the production needs of all those involved. Resources for access might be similarly pooled to avoid unnecessary and expensive duplication. Such cooperative efforts may prove to be doubly beneficial for municipalities that are similar in character or that have a history of mutual activities to reinforce existing ties or create new ones.

Some feel that one drawback to interconnecting community channels is that it may remove the local character of the channels. They may also feel that pooling resources in one location may make access equipment less accessible to residents of the other communities. However, this need not be the case. Through careful scheduling and educational efforts, the access staff can assure that all communities are actively involved. Portable access equipment "packages" can be placed in individual communities so that distance from the central facility does not deter community participation.

Institutional users   Institutional users of cable systems have a great deal to gain from interconnected channels. Often such users provide services to audiences that are not contained within a single franchise district. In other cases, similar institutions in different franchise districts may offer the same service. In either instance, interconnected channels can help deliver these services in a more efficient and cost-effective manner.

A good example of an institutional application of interconnection is the distribution of higher education materials. By interconnecting an educational channel among many systems, it is possible to extend educational offerings to many students efficiently. And, as with community programming, interconnection could help facilitate pooling of resources among institutions and make these educational services more cost-effective.

Modern cable systems frequently provide for a separate institutional cable that is used to link local institutions, agencies, and businesses. The interconnection of systems can help extend and enhance the kinds of services being offered through this kind of local loop. For instance, interconnecting the institutional loops of several systems can make it possible for all health agencies within a region to share materials. In addition to the cost savings, interconnection can contribute uniformity to area-wide information and training programs.

More and more institutions are beginning to explore the possibilities for data transfer via cable. They include local governments and libraries as well as education, health, and business institutions. Particularly in large metropolitan areas there may be a need to move data from city to nearby city. This kind of information transfer is frequently accomplished via phone lines. However, interconnected adjacent cable systems are another option.

Benefits to the system operator   A key benefit of interconnection as seen by cable operators is the possibility of increasing revenues by attracting advertising support. National and regional advertisers frequently have bypassed cable because they would have to negotiate with several operators to reach a sufficiently large audience. Through system interconnection, larger audiences are possible, and potential revenues are equally large. Gill Cable's interconnect in San Jose, California (described later), helped the system earn approximately $1 million in advertising revenues during 1980.[1] A new interconnect in Connecticut was estimated to have generated $100,000 over a three-month period.

Cable operators can profit from the opportunity to share the costs of staff, services, and equipment. The advantages of sharing local origination and access costs have already been described. Some of the other programming most in demand by subscribers is provided to operators via satellite. When systems are interconnected, satellite dishes (which can range in cost from $5,000 to $10,000) can be shared and jointly financed.

Operators may also find that interconnection makes it possible to offer new kinds of services. Such offerings as home banking and home shopping may become economically viable only when large numbers of subscribers can be served.

As with public service users, some commercial cable users may have a service with broad appeal to offer. Newspapers, for example, are experimenting with text information channels that could command regional audiences. Other commercial users, such as banks, might need to transfer data from one municipality to another. The potential for economic benefit is strong; for that reason, the private sector is likely to give serious attention to interconnected systems in the future.

Interconnection configurations   There are several different levels of system interconnection. The first is the municipal level. The typical pattern across the country is one cable company operating in one community. In a few larger cities, however, several companies serve separate subdistricts. For these communities, the issue of interconnection is especially relevant, because interconnection is necessary to disseminate citywide information efficiently.

Beyond that, interconnections can be developed on a regional basis. Perhaps most likely is the linking of systems within a metropolitan area (for example, a city with surrounding suburbs). However, countywide and even statewide interconnections are also developing. National interconnection of systems is possible, though economically feasible only with satellite technology.

Ownership and management options

It is fairly easy to identify potential uses and users of interconnected cable systems. But ownership and management structures are much more complicated because both touch on the sensitive issues of access to and control of the overall communication system.

There are three basic options for ownership of the interconnection technology: private ownership, public ownership, or some combination of the two. The existing interconnections are largely privately owned. In some cases, a single operator has financed the hardware, whereas in others participating cable companies have split the costs. Management has followed the same pattern, with either a single system assuming responsibilities, or with participants acting jointly. Sometimes an entirely separate corporation has been set up to manage the interconnect on behalf of all participating operators.

Public ownership of an interconnection has been virtually untested. However, it would seem an ideal approach if the primary goal of the interconnection is to deliver nonprofit public services. Municipalities might jointly own the interconnect, a separate nonprofit corporation might be established, or an existing State or regional agency might become involved. The specific options for a given area depend on the kinds of arrangements permitted under State and local laws.

Initial financing of a public interconnection could take several forms. Participating municipalities might each be assessed a share of the costs, or grant monies might be available. Given the pressures on local government budgets and competition for grants, however, these options may prove problematic. Another approach might be to issue municipal bonds. But again, some careful legal research would be necessary to determine what is permissible in a particular location. Joint public and private financing is also an option, subject to State and local laws.

Under public ownership, municipalities are unlikely to have the expertise needed to run an interconnect effectively. Thus the question of management is an important one. The kinds of functions that need to be performed include maintaining and upgrading the interconnect equipment, scheduling use of the system, promoting services, cablecasting programming, and carrying out other day-to-day operations. Participating cities can hire staff, but another approach might be to work out a separate management scheme by contracting with professional communication companies or arranging with participating cable companies to handle operational functions.

Whatever the ownership structure, an important issue is control of access to the system. Another issue is the use to which it may be put. Should the owner of the hardware be the gatekeeper? And if the owner retains control, what guarantees are there that both commercial and noncommercial services will develop? These questions are just beginning to come into public focus.

A new kind of ownership and management structure that has begun to emerge is a separate body that provides the interconnection and makes the channels available to both commercial and noncommercial users. The company recoups its costs by charging fees to users. Such an interconnection may be operated on a common carrier basis (i.e., universal access to channels, with a posted set of rates), thus eliminating problems of access to and control over the system.

Interconnection technology

Essentially, interconnection is a matter of distributing cable signals from one headend to another. Two basic types of technology can be used for interconnection: coaxial or fiber wire and broadcast technology. The selection of the technology depends on several factors, including distance, the terrain, number of channels, type of application, and availability of frequencies.

Broadcast technology, or "over-the-air," interconnection is usually accomplished using microwave radio. Microwave transmitters and receivers can send and receive several cable channels from cable headend to headend. A multichannel transmitter is more cost-effective when many channels are to be interconnected, and the most sophisticated can handle up to 54 channels.

An alternative is coaxial cable interconnection. However, cable is expensive to lay down and thus is not considered cost-effective except when relatively short distances between interconnection points are to be covered (5 to 10 miles). Cable interconnection does not require licensing or spectrum availability, as does microwave.

Fiber optics and satellites are other potential interconnection technologies. Fiber optics is still considered experimental and is not frequently proposed for cable system interconnection. Satellites are expensive for regional interconnections, and are normally used to carry national signals intended for national distribution.

Regulation of interconnections

Perhaps the most challenging aspects of cable system interconnection are the regulatory questions. In the past, cable systems have been regulated at the Federal, State, and local levels. As cable technology has changed, new policy issues have surfaced and governments have struggled to cope with them. Because interconnections typically cross jurisdictional lines, they add still another layer of complexity to these policy questions.

To date, a limited number of regulations directly address or affect interconnection. At the municipal level, provisions dealing with easements and public rights-of-way would affect the laying of any wire technology incorporated into the interconnection. Likewise, microwave towers might be subject to local zoning laws, depending on their placement.

Franchising authorities are becoming sensitive to the need to address the question of interconnection, not an easy task. In drafting a request for proposals (RFP), a city is in a position to deal with only one component of an interconnection. Operators responding to an RFP are in a position to promise only what

they individually are able to do. In the absence of State requirements for interconnection, cities and operators must rely on
cooperation and coordination to see the interconnection concept
implemented.

Some cities have begun including interconnection provisions in their franchise ordinances, particularly cities that have
more than one cable company operating within their boundaries.
Seattle, a city with five franchise districts, in a recent franchise
award has required the franchisee to interconnect the access
channel within 18 months after the award. Both Phoenix (another city with multiple systems) and Cincinnati have required
their franchisees to interconnect at the request of the city.

At the State level, the subject of interconnection remains
relatively untouched. As might be expected, States that have
addressed interconnection are those that already play a strong
role in cable regulation and development.

One of the strongest stances has been taken by Minnesota.
In 1973, the Minnesota legislature created the Minnesota Cable
Communications Board to oversee the development and regulation of cable. Within the enabling legislation were sections that
called on the board to

... prescribe standards for: franchises awarded in the twin cities
metropolitan area which designates a uniform regional channel; the
interconnection of all cable systems within this area; and the designation of a single entity to schedule programs and facilitate use of
this channel;
... designate the entity referred to in clause (c) and prescribe rules
for its operation and practice which rules shall insure that priority is
given to public use of the uniform regional channel.
... Subd. 12. The board shall prescribe standards for interconnection and compatibility of cable communications systems.[2]

A set of administrative rules for cable systems later evolved
that addressed interconnection more comprehensively. These
required that all cable systems within the 7-county metropolitan
area of Minneapolis-St. Paul must interconnect on standard
VHF channel 6 to create a uniform "regional channel." The rules
further required the board to designate a regional channel
"entity" to schedule the programming and facilitate use of the
channel. They also specified technical standards for interconnection within the State.

As this article was being written, the Minnesota Cable
Communications Board was in the process of implementing the
interconnection requirements. Many policy questions were being discussed, including the potential uses of the regional channel, who should be designated as the regional channel entity,
procedures for interconnection, access to the interconnection
system, and financing and management questions.

A similar plan is evolving in Rhode Island. In January 1981 the Division of Public Utilities and Carriers of the Public Utilities Commission adopted rules governing cable communications systems that included a section on interconnection of systems. This section required that:

1. All systems to be designed and constructed so they are capable of interconnecting with adjacent systems.
2. Within 18 months after two or more systems receive authorization from the State to operate they should interconnect and begin providing programming. Other systems are also required to do the same within 18 months after certification.
3. The statewide interconnection should be capable of both upstream and downstream signals and at least two upstream and two downstream channels should be interconnected.
4. Operators are required to pay a proportionate share of establishing and running the interconnection.

Like Minnesota, Rhode Island envisions that some entity will have to be set up to oversee the use of the interconnect; however, the administrative details have not been worked out.

Two other States that have addressed interconnection are New York and Massachusetts. In the enabling legislation that created the New York State Commission on Cable Television there are provisions that require systems to be technically capable of interconnecting and that give the commission authority to order interconnection whenever it finds it to be in the public interest. Thus far, the commission has not ordered interconnection. Agency staff have compiled a statewide inventory of microwave and satellite facilities that might be used for interconnection and have included interconnection as a goal in the statewide development plan.

The Massachusetts cable regulations make no mention of interconnection, but the Massachusetts Cable Commission is beginning to study the subject for informational purposes. They see their ongoing role as one of facilitating interconnection. To date, they have no plans to promulgate interconnection regulations of any kind.

A final State that has taken some initiative with interconnection is New Jersey. Intrigued with the potential of statewide interconnection for public service uses of cable, the Office of Cable Television in the Board of Public Utilities began feasibility studies of statewide interconnection in 1979. The agency foresaw that the State's community colleges might be able to deliver educational programming over such a system. It hoped to play a key role in the development and management of the interconnect.

Agency representatives went ahead and obtained the necessary microwave licenses but were unable to proceed further. The Treasury Department of the State of New Jersey raised questions about the legality of the State becoming involved in an interconnection scheme. On February 19, 1980, the State Attorney General's office issued an opinion that the Office of Cable Television could not be involved in the construction, supervision, or maintenance of an interconnection or use State assessments (fees paid to the State by cable companies) for interconnection. The attorney general found that it was beyond the scope of the agency's jurisdiction to play such an active role.

The Office of Cable Television has since turned over its microwave licenses to industry representatives and is encouraging companies to make public interest programming a priority in any interconnection that is developed. This experience suggests that regulatory agencies in other States should think carefully about how they become involved with interconnection.

At the Federal level, interconnection is currently effected through the licensing of microwave and satellite frequencies. Beyond that, the FCC has developed no policies but rather is adopting a "wait and see" attitude. Similarly, Congress has not become involved in interconnection issues.

There is some potential for additional regulatory activity at both the State and Federal levels. Relatively few of a system's total channels are likely to be interconnected in any given situation. Thus, a scarce resource (regional channels) is being created within a technology of supposed "nonscarcity." Because the demand for regional channels could be great, questions about access to those channels and priority uses may be raised. Scarcity traditionally has been used as a rationale to regulate broadcasting.

Similarly, interconnections may take on certain monopolistic characteristics. The availability of microwave frequencies and other technical considerations may make it difficult for more than one interconnection scheme to be developed for a given set of systems. This may put interconnected channels in the hands of a single entity, with little chance for competition.

The lack of competition could become a critical issue if fees become associated with interconnection. At present, interconnections have not involved charges for channel time. As the applications expand, however, and as common carrier or lease schemes are initiated, questions are likely to be raised about rate regulation.

It is important to note here that when systems are interconnected, an entirely new communications avenue is created—one that does not fit neatly within traditional boundaries. Up until now, governments at the State, local, and Federal levels have each claimed a role in overseeing cable. But interconnected systems straddle the lines between each level of government, making a regional body of some kind seem a more likely choice. Such bodies do not now exist, and whether it is possible or advisable to create a fourth tier of regulation in an era of deregulation is a topic for considerable thought and discussion.

Summary

Although the future of interconnections seems promising, an array of questions have yet to be fully addressed. Depending on how they are resolved, interconnections could spread widely or develop only sporadically.

Some of the larger questions are related to access, control, ownership, and regulation. But others are equally significant. For example, because of the state of the economy, most interconnections will be financed privately rather than publicly. If companies foot the bill, can they or should they be required to provide for public service users? And to what extent can the industry be expected to subsidize institutions, agencies, and governments that wish to use interconnected channels but cannot contribute to hardware costs?

Still another important issue is whether interconnection can proceed on a scale that may be desirable. Many systems in the country still have limited channel capacity, and such systems may not be able to make bandwidth available for interconnection even if they want to. Smaller systems may not be able to afford the costs of interconnection technology and so may be left out of interconnection schemes. Finally, interconnection may be slowed because of various tiering and rate schemes being used. Channels may be available on different tiers in different systems, so efforts to share services may prove to be awkward.

1. Susan Spillman, "Interconnects: The Numbers Game," *CableVision*, March 9, 1981, p. 41.

2. Minn. Stat., Chapter 238.05, subd. 2(c & d) and 12.